Ms. Wood's Wild

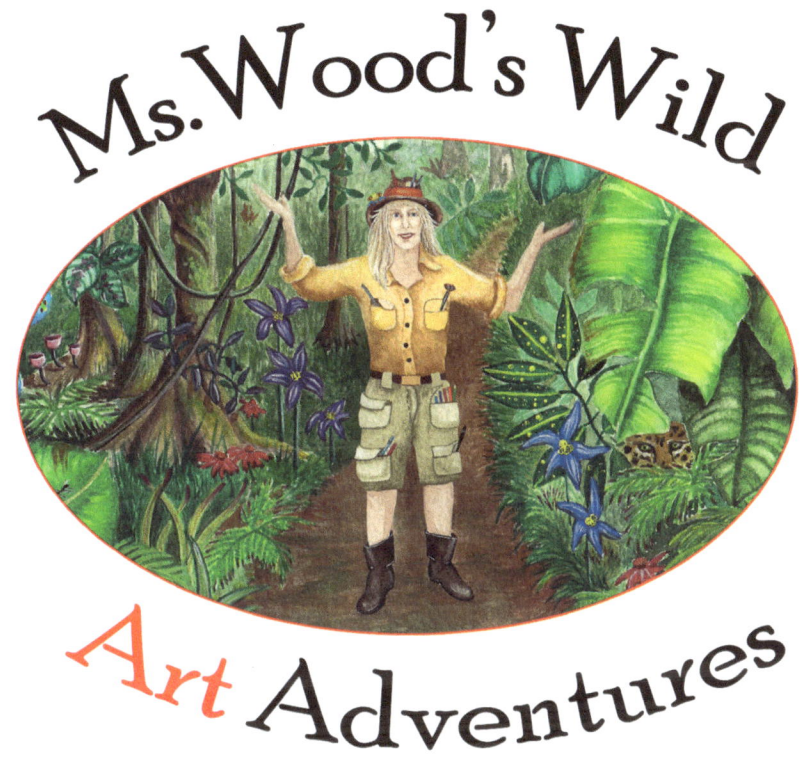

Art Adventures

THE RAINFOREST

Written & Illustrated by
Jan Wood Harris

Dedicated to each and every student I've taught along the way.
This path has truly been a Wild Art Adventure!
This book is a gift to you... in return for
all that you have given me over the years.

Thank you to my wonderfull and loving family. Their
support and encouragement through my years of teaching
and through the creation of this book,
will forever be cherished.

Published with CreateSpace, an Amazon Company - Independent Publishing

ISBN 10: 1480255769
ISBN 13: 978-1480255760

INTRODUCTION.......

Children have such rich imaginations and are always telling their own stories through their drawings. Through these imaginations, much can be learned. So it just made sense to combine art instruction and education with simple story-telling in this charming, richly illustrated book series.

Apart from wanting the reader/student to learn the fundamentals of art, my goal is to create a sense of joy connected to art with no stress, and more self discovery.

In this book series, I take the reader/student on Art Adventures into many different environments full of visual goodies, if you will, reinforcing observation of the world around them in ways they hadn't considered before. Then, through this new awareness, comes an excitement to capture this in their own artwork.

Most importantly, my hope is that the reader/student discovers within themselves a new-found confidence and fearlessness that comes from being equipped with evolving knowledge, techniques and abilities. This confidence enhances their creativity and imagination in their artwork, and these wonderful attributes expand into other parts of their lives as well!

Jan Wood Harris

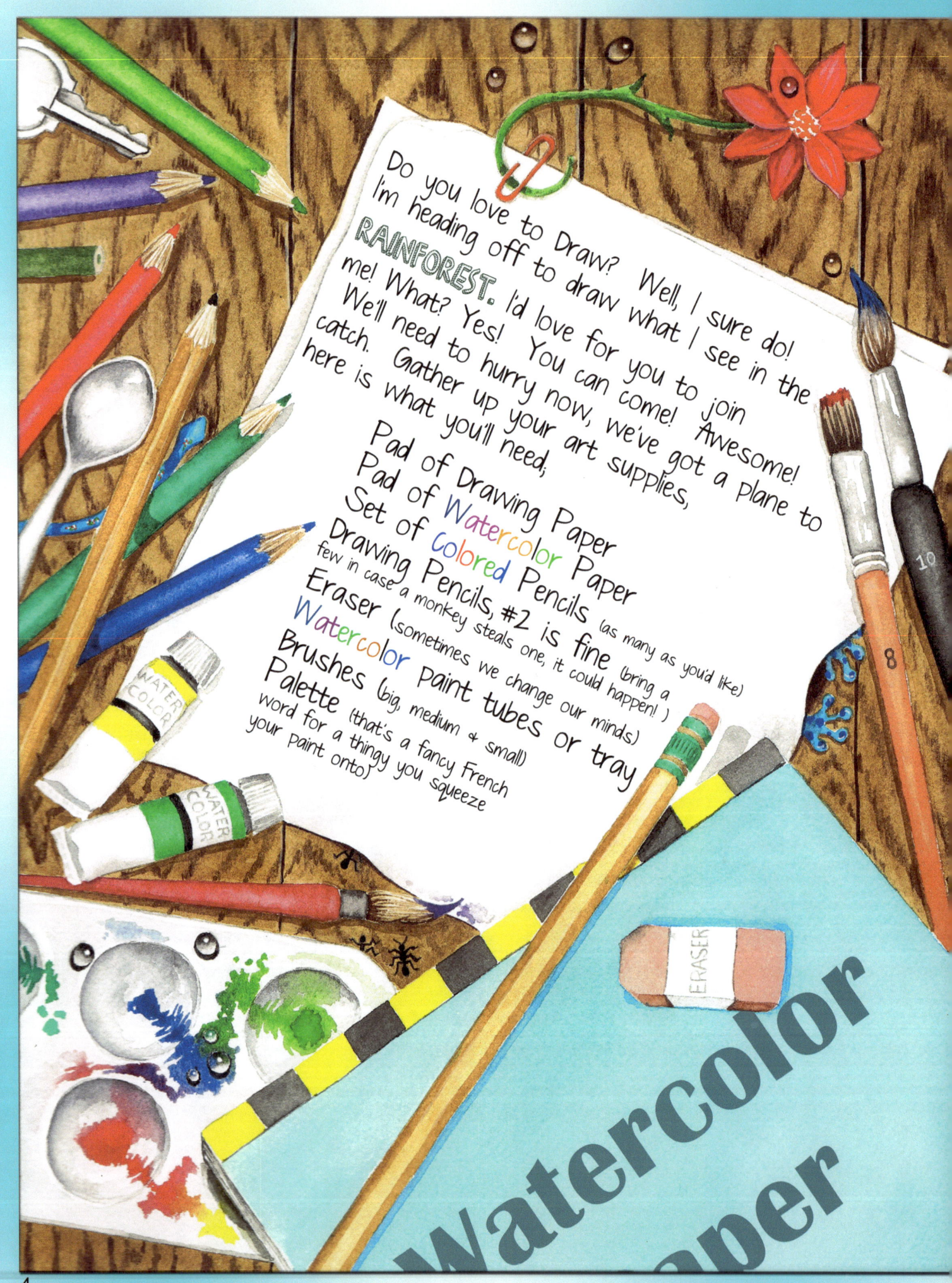

Do you love to Draw? Well, I sure do! I'm heading off to draw what I see in the RAINFOREST. I'd love for you to join me! What? Yes! You can come! Awesome! We'll need to hurry now, we've got a plane to catch. Gather up your art supplies, here is what you'll need;

Pad of Drawing Paper
Pad of Watercolor Paper
Set of Colored Pencils (as many as you'd like)
Drawing Pencils, #2 is fine (bring a few in case a monkey steals one, it could happen!)
Eraser (sometimes we change our minds)
Watercolor Paint tubes or tray
Brushes (big, medium & small)
Palette (that's a fancy French word for a thingy you squeeze your paint onto)

Watercolor
paper

4

We made it, and you've got the window seat! LUCKY YOU! LOOK out the window at those beautiful FLUFFY WHITE CLOUDS !

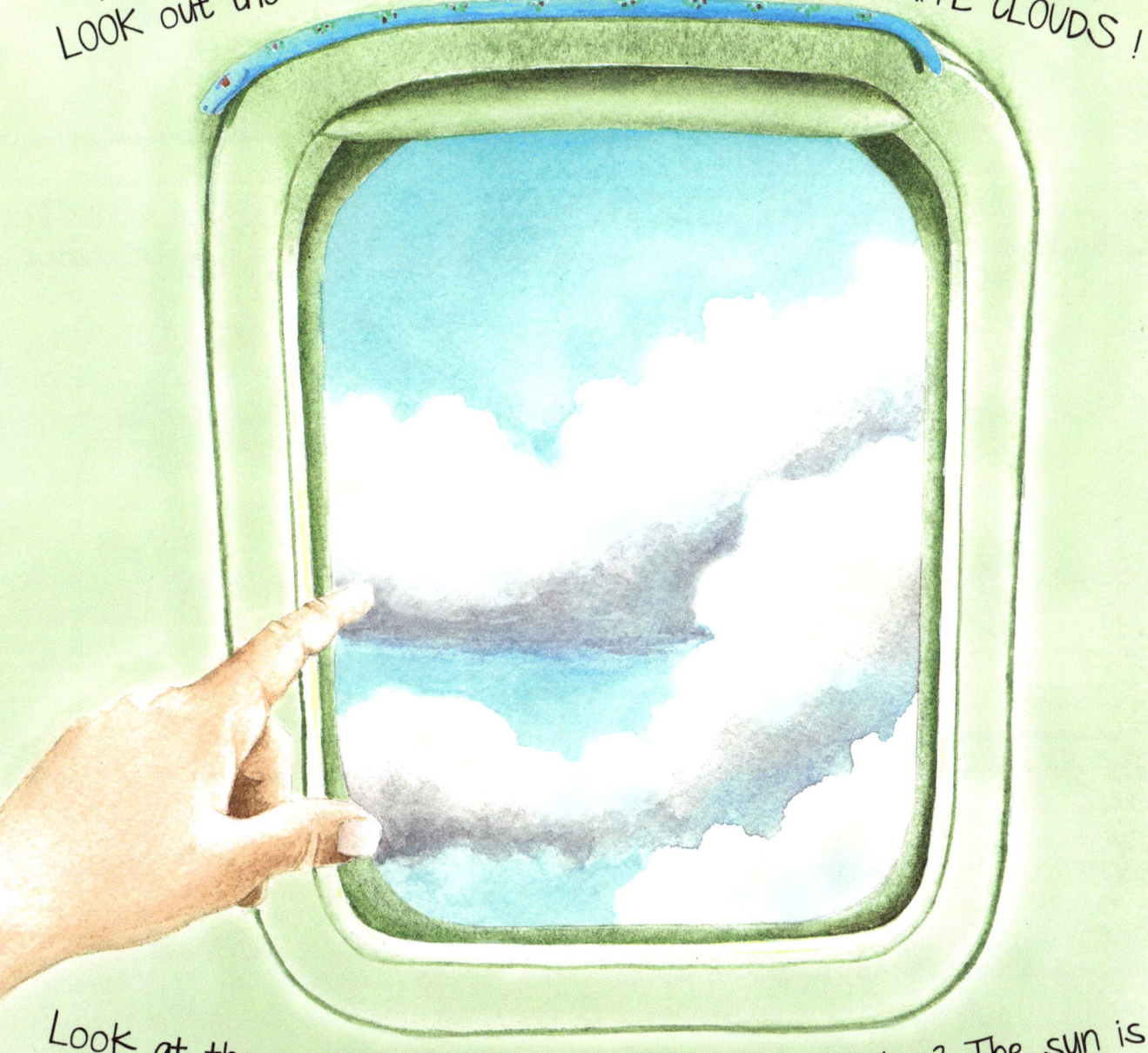

Look at them again! They're not just white, are they? The sun is above the clouds, so the top is bright WHITE from the sun's LIGHT, with a touch of YELLOW from the sun and BLUE reflecting the blue sky.

Underneath are shades of GRAY & PURPLE because there is little sunlight there, so it makes a SHADOW under the clouds. I'll ask the nice flight attendent to bring us some water and let's

☆ PAINT WHAT WE SEE ☆

LET'S PAINT SOME CLOUDS!

NEEDED: Palette, Brush, Watercolor paper, & water. Paint: Blue, Red & Golden-Yellow.

Before we start painting, let's have all our paint in our palette and ready to go! Squeeze a bit of blue, red and golden yellow into separate 'bowls' in our palette. Now, let's add water to each color with our brush until it's the color we want. (More water=lighter color, less water=darker color). In a separate 'bowl' on our palette let's mix a bit of blue and red together to make light purple.

Ok, ready, set.... Let's **PAINT WHAT WE SEE** ! *

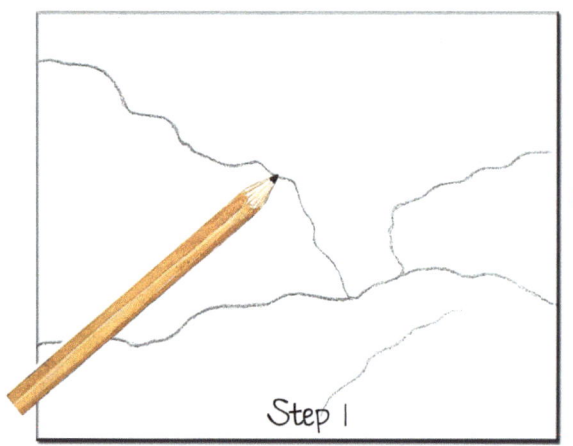

Step 1

First, with our pencil, lightly out-line where we want the tops of our clouds to be. Remember, draw very lightly so we don't see our pencil lines through our paint. Perfect!

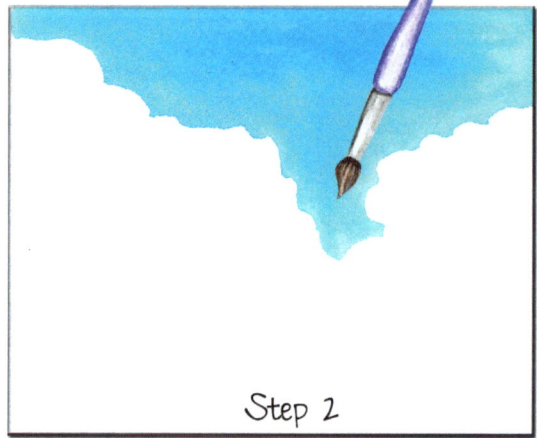

Step 2

Next, let's take our wet brush and dip it into our blue paint. Starting from the top of the page let's paint the blue right down to our pencil line. Good job!

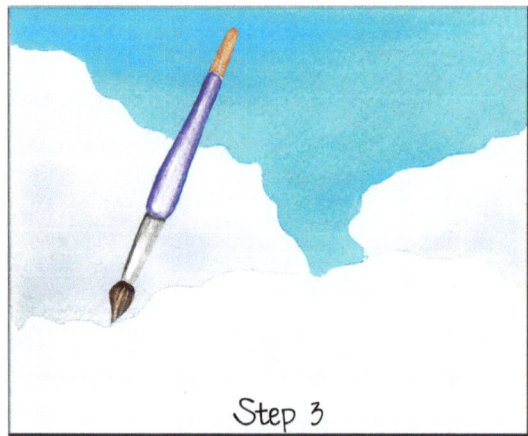

Step 3

Now let's rinse the blue off our brush in clean water. Let's dip our clean wet brush into the purple paint we made by mixing the blue and red together. Very lightly paint the 'shadow' on the clouds, from inside the cloud down to the line of the lower cloud.

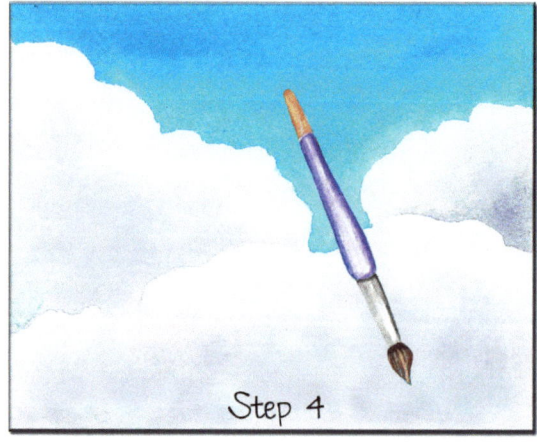

Step 4

Continue with painting the purple along the bottom of the lower cloud. Let's be careful to leave the top part of our clouds un-painted. (just below our pencil line) We want the clouds to look fluffy white on top. Remember the light from the sun!

* Remember, if you don't have paint in tubes, paint trays are great to use too!

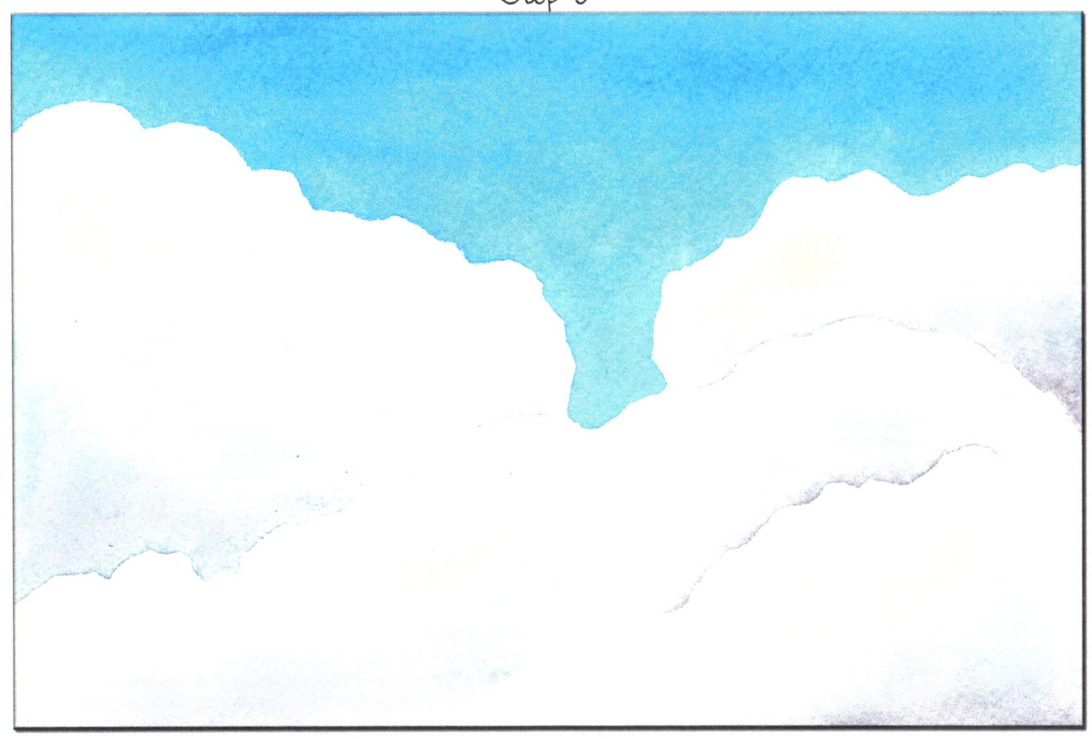

Now let's finish up our beautiful fluffy white clouds! Let's rinse our brushes
with clean water and dip it into the golden-yellow paint, just a little now!
Then very lightly paint a 'soft' amount onto the middle of our clouds.
They're done! Good Job !

Below I've painted examples of works by three Master Artists who also
like to paint clouds. These artists all paint in different 'styles', which means
they see things in their own way and then
paint how they see it !

VINCENT VAN GOGH 1853-1890
Dutch
Look at his painting
'Wheat Fields with Cypresses'

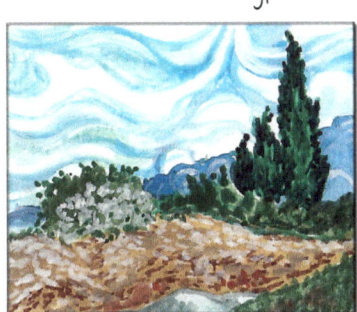

Vincent Van Gogh sees clouds
as colored spirals moving in crazy
patterns up in the sky.
His style is called IMPRESSIONISM

JOHN CONSTABLE 1776-1837
English
Look at his painting
'Wivenhoe Park'

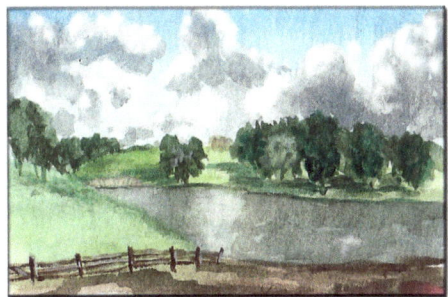

John Constable sees clouds
pretty much as they truly are in
a perfect beautiful landscape..
His style is called ROMANTIC REALISM

GEORGIA O'KEEFFE 1887-1986
American
Look at her painting
'Sky Above the Clouds'

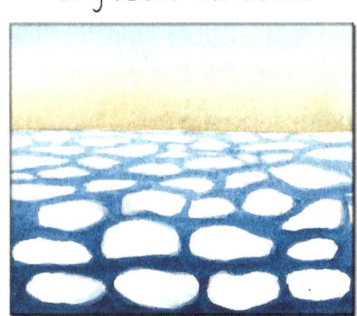

Georgia O'Keeffe sees clouds as
big, flat white circles
in a bright blue sky.
Her style is called MODERN ART

These 3 works of art are painted by Jan Wood Harris in a style similar to the paintings listed.

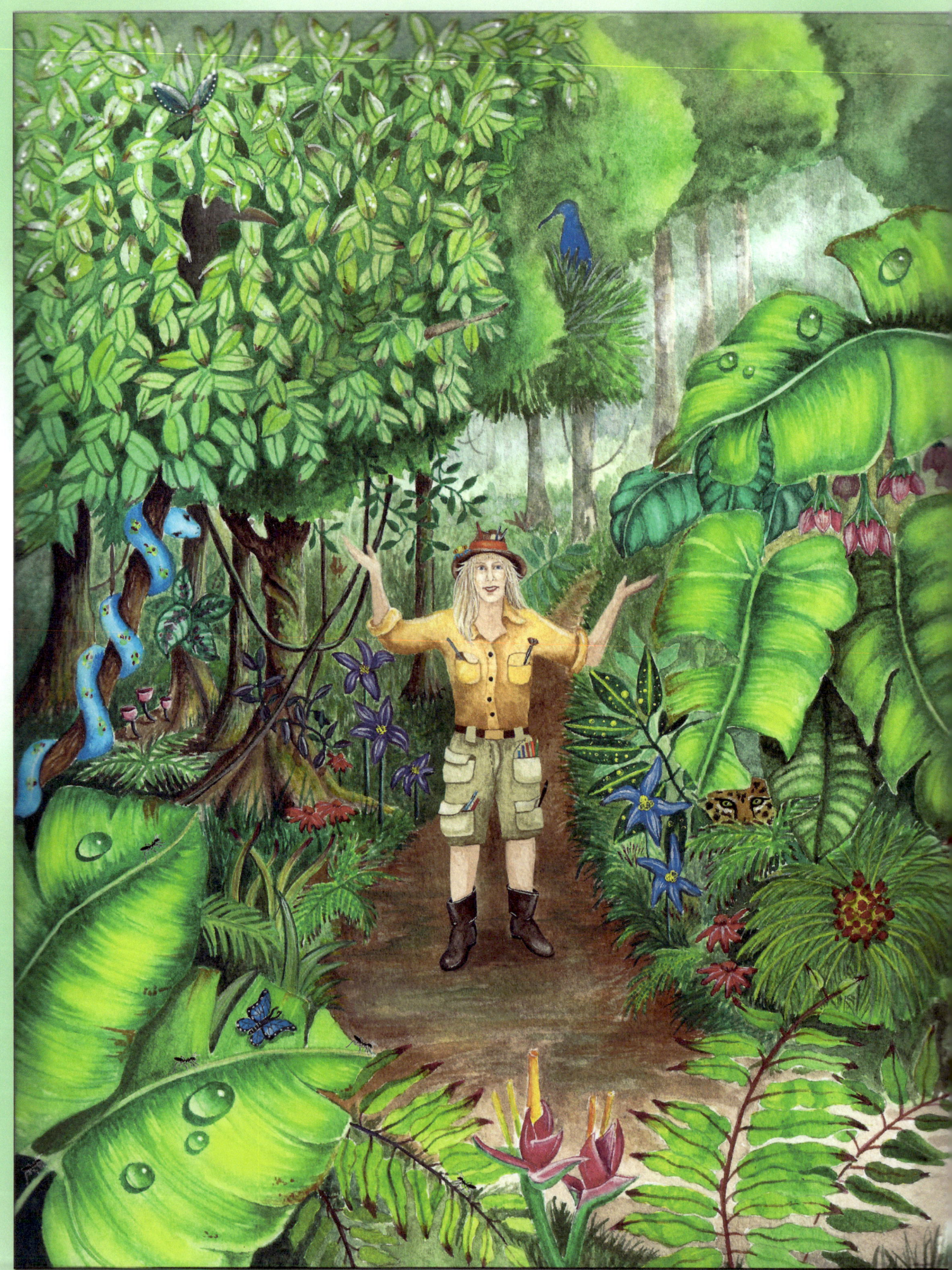

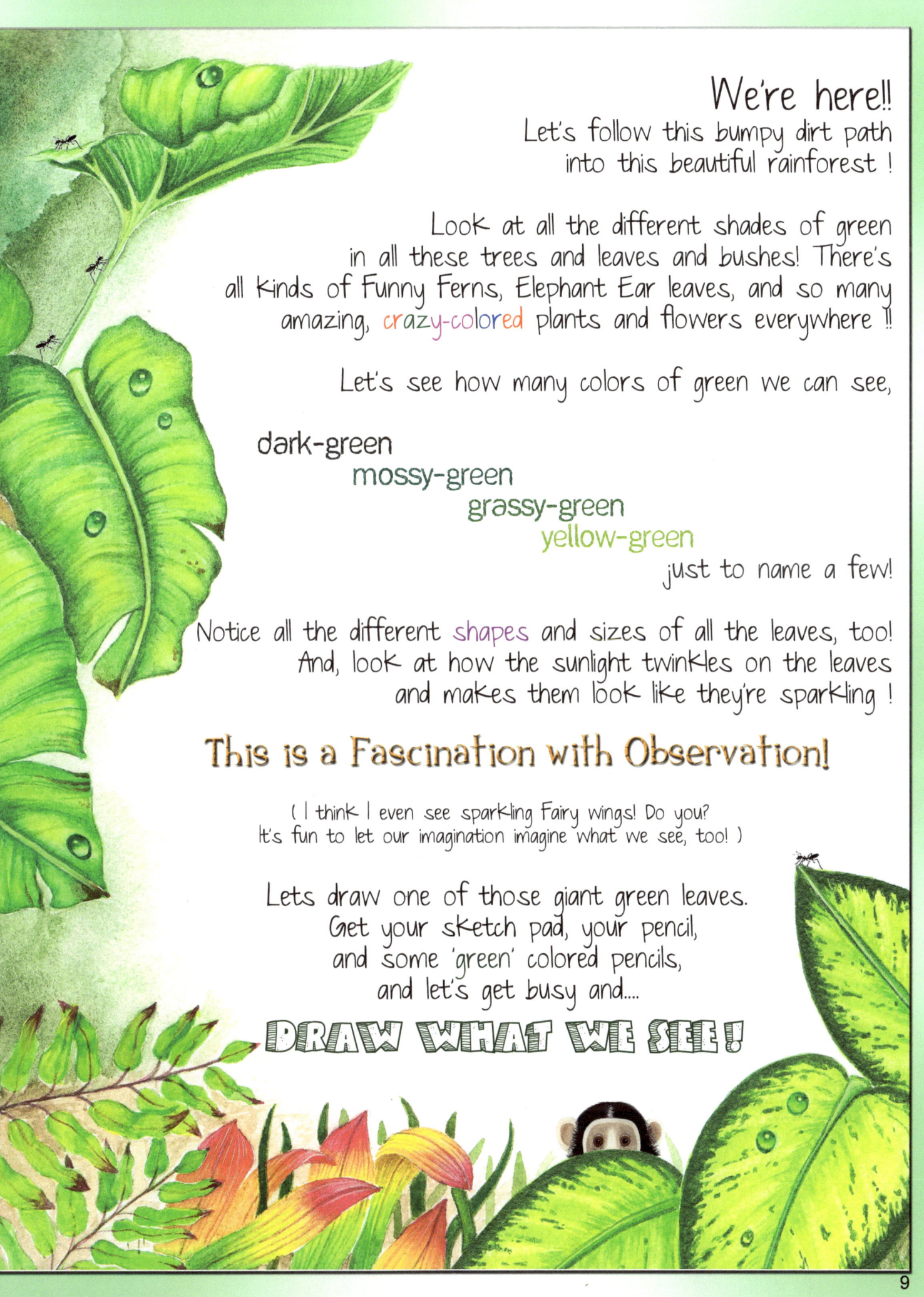

We're here!!

Let's follow this bumpy dirt path
into this beautiful rainforest !

Look at all the different shades of green
in all these trees and leaves and bushes! There's
all kinds of Funny Ferns, Elephant Ear leaves, and so many
amazing, crazy-colored plants and flowers everywhere !!

Let's see how many colors of green we can see,

dark-green
mossy-green
grassy-green
yellow-green

just to name a few!

Notice all the different shapes and sizes of all the leaves, too!
And, look at how the sunlight twinkles on the leaves
and makes them look like they're sparkling !

This is a Fascination with Observation!

(I think I even see sparkling Fairy wings! Do you?
It's fun to let our imagination imagine what we see, too!)

Lets draw one of those giant green leaves.
Get your sketch pad, your pencil,
and some 'green' colored pencils,
and let's get busy and....

DRAW WHAT WE SEE !

LET'S DRAW A TROPICAL LEAF!

NEEDED: Colored Pencils; a dark-green, a yellow-green and a yellow.

Before we start drawing, let's make sure that all our pencils have been sharpened! Next, we'll need a sheet of drawing paper to start this project.

OK, looks like we have everything! Let's **DRAW WHAT WE SEE!**

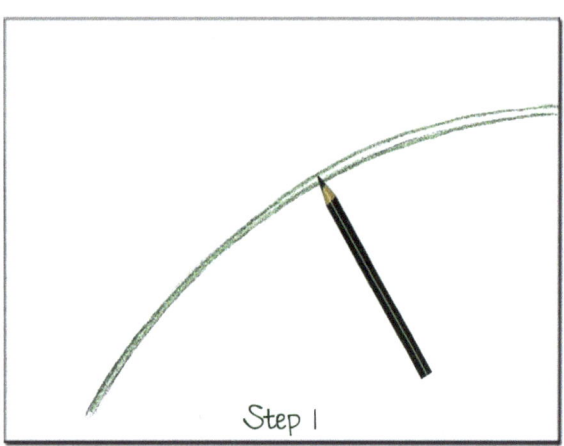

Step 1

First, with our dark green pencil let's draw the center of the leaf. Notice the curve of the line and that it gets a little skinnier towards the tip of the leaf.

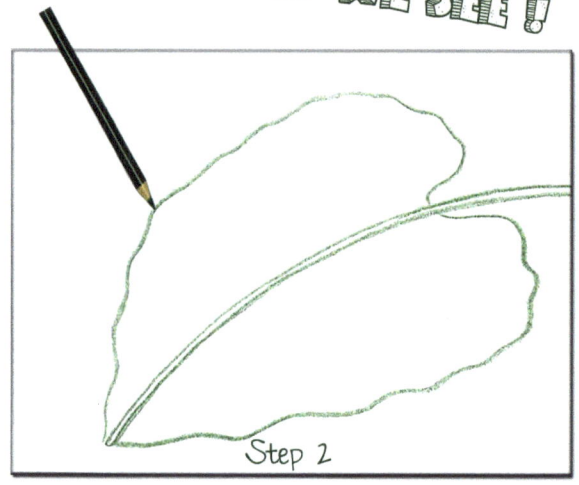

Step 2

Next, still using our dark green pencil, let's draw the outer edges of the leaf. It almost looks like a wobbly heart shape, doesn't it!

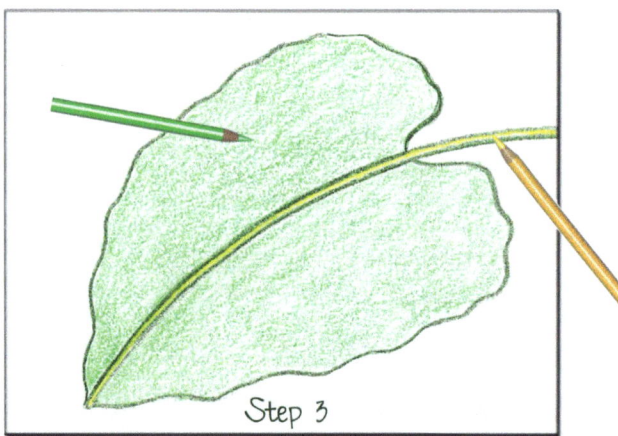

Step 3

Now, let's take our yellow-green pencil and start to fill in the inside of our leaf. Be sure to stay inside our lines and try and draw the green as evenly as you can. Add a little yellow to the stem.

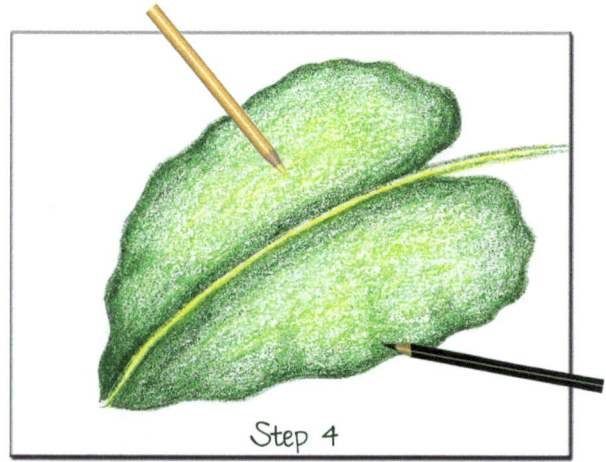

Step 4

With our dark green pencil again, let's add some 'shading' around the edges of the leaf and on either side of the center line of the leaf. Then, with our yellow pencil, let's add a little yellow to the top of our leaf to show sunlight.

Green colored pencils have so many different names, just pick 3 that best match these colors, whatever their names are!

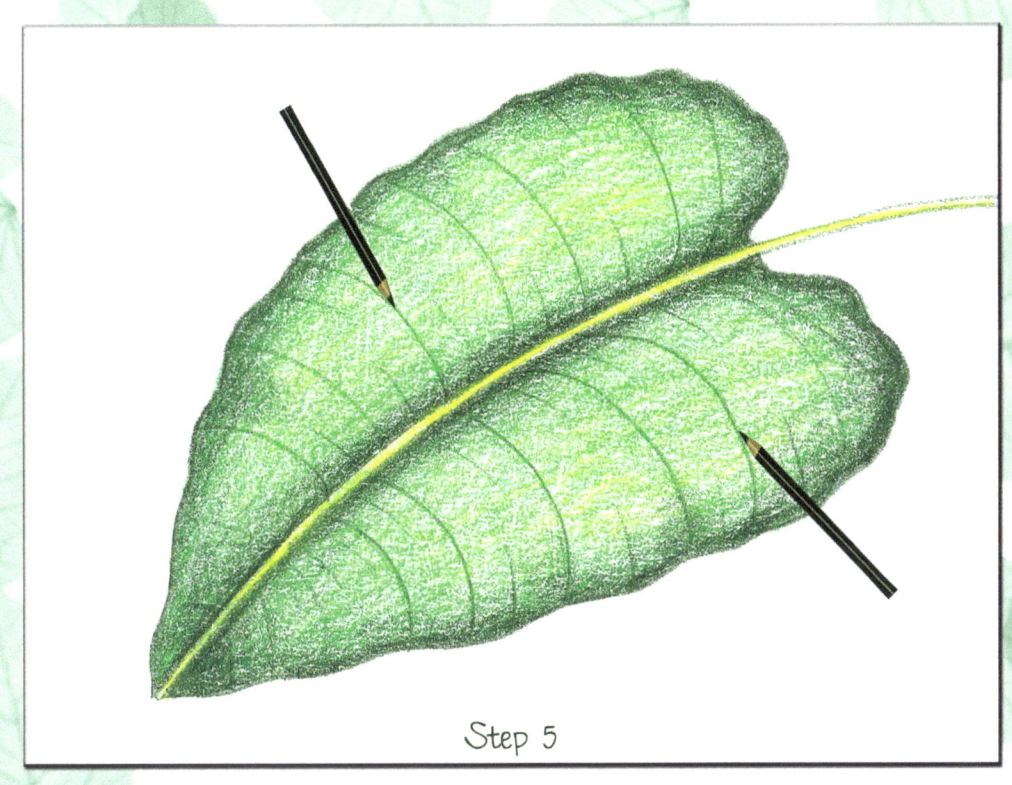

Step 5

Finally, to finish up our beautiful Tropical leaf, let's add some detail ! With our dark green pencil let's draw some 'vein' lines on our leaf. We are going to draw these lines slightly curved because the leaf is curved! These are called 'contour lines'! These lines help to show the curvature of the leaf. You can use this technique when you try and draw your own tropical forest too !

☆

Below I've painted examples of artwork by three Master Artists who also like to paint leaves and forest scenes. These artists all paint in different art 'styles', which means they see things in their own way and then paint how they see it !

HENRI ROUSSEAU 1844-1910
French
Look at his painting;
'Woman walking in an exotic forest'.

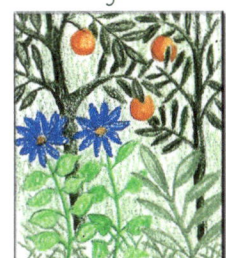

Rousseau sees plants as simple forms, almost childlike. His style is POST IMPRESSIONIST 'PRIMITIVE STYLE'

GUSTAV KLIMT 1862-1918
Austrian
Look at his painting
'Tree of Life III'

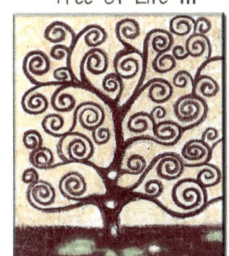

Gustav Klimt saw the tree as a symbol of life with its trunk & many branches. His style is SYMBOLISM

GEORGE SEURAT 1859-1891
French
Look at his painting
The Seine at la Grande Jatte

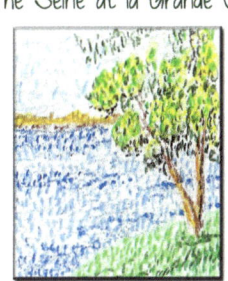

Seurat sees plants & trees as smalls dots or as points of color. His style is IMPRESSIONISM 'POINTILLISM'

These 3 works of art are painted by Jan Wood Harris in a style similar to the paintings listed.

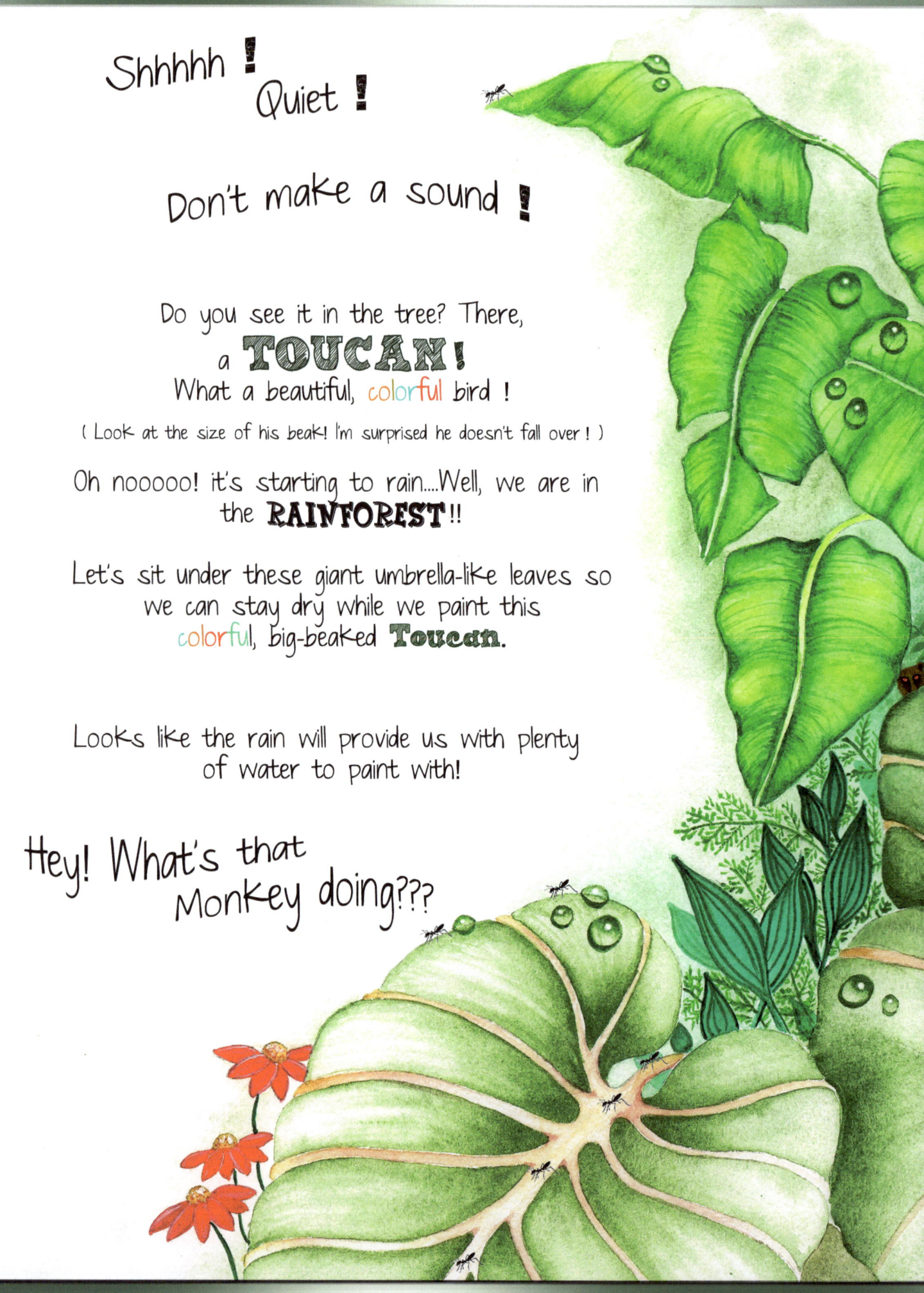

Shhhh ! Quiet !

Don't make a sound !

Do you see it in the tree? There,
a **TOUCAN!**
What a beautiful, colorful bird !

(Look at the size of his beak! I'm surprised he doesn't fall over !)

Oh nooooo! it's starting to rain....Well, we are in
the **RAINFOREST**!!

Let's sit under these giant umbrella-like leaves so
we can stay dry while we paint this
colorful, big-beaked **Toucan**.

Looks like the rain will provide us with plenty
of water to paint with!

Hey! What's that
Monkey doing???

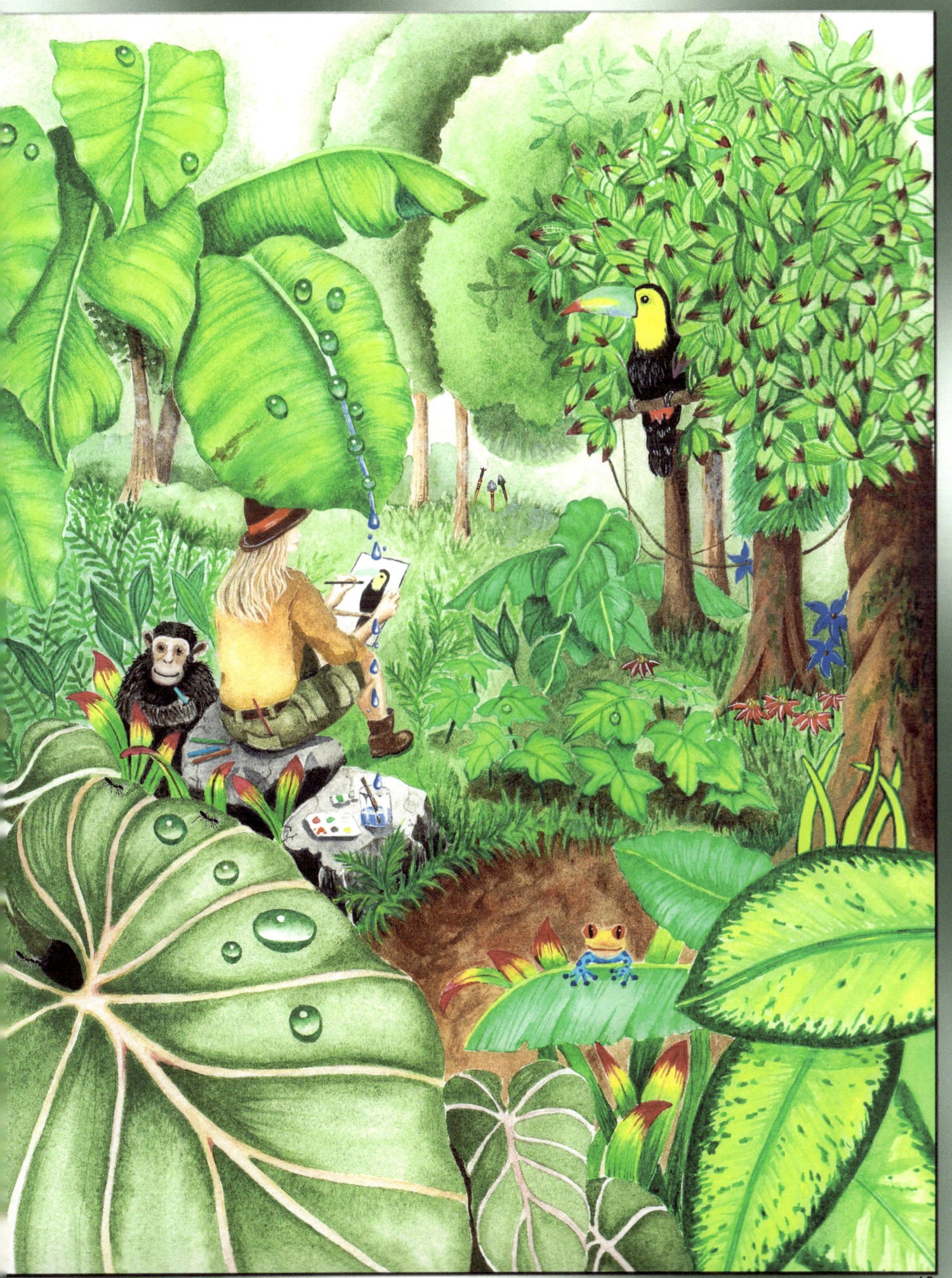

LET'S PAINT A TOUCAN !

NEEDED: Watercolor paper, palette, brush, water. Paint: black, yellow, blue, green, brown, golden (mix brown/yellow), red, aqua (mix blue/green), and gray.

Follow the same instructions for setting up our paint palette when we painted the clouds, only with these paint colors. So, let's grab a pencil and start to **PAINT WHAT WE SEE!**

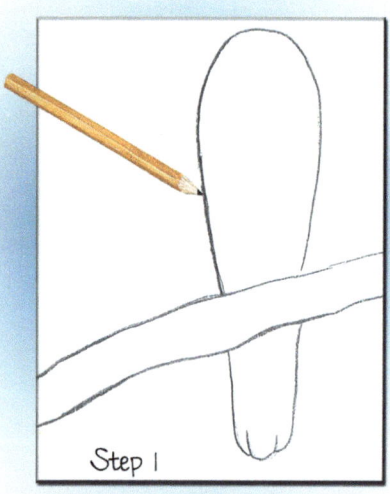

Step 1

For the tree branch, start drawing low on your paper to allow room for the Toucan on top. Next, draw a big 'Loop' on top of the branch, then a smaller 'loop' under the branch for the Toucan's tail.

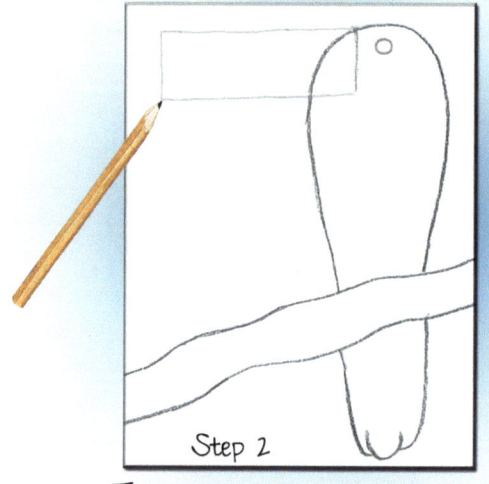

Step 2

This next step is an easy one! We are going to draw a faint rectangle where we want the Toucan's big beak to go. Draw a small circle for the eye.

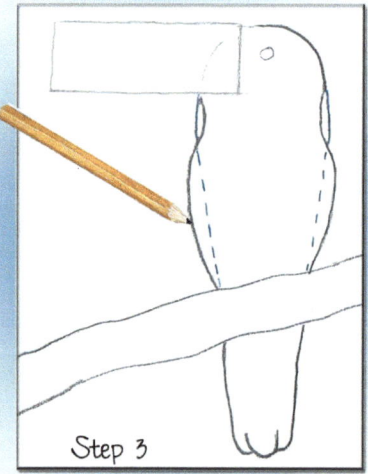

Step 3

Let's give our Toucan a little shape. The original line we made is in blue dashes. Let's bring our line in to make a neck, then poof it out to show our Toucan's chest.

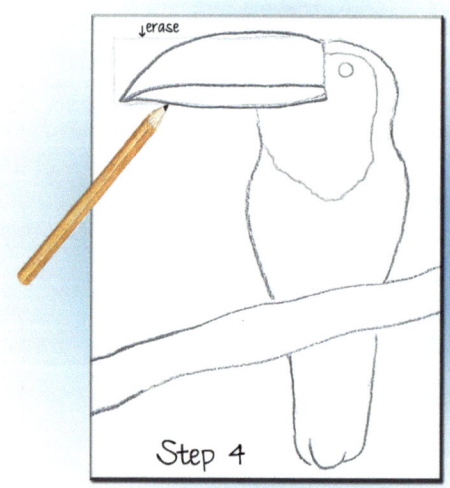

erase

Step 4

Now let's draw the line that starts above the eye then down on his chest (where the yellow feathers go!) For the beak, follow how the lines go within the rectangle that we drew previously.

Your **Toucan** is looking great! Next step, we start to paint and add his feet !!

Next, using golden, paint the branch 'lenghthwise'. With the brown, paint the bottom half in short, chunky strokes. This gives a 'bark-like' 'texture'.

The golden shows 'light' on top of the branch. The brown shows a 'shadow' along the bottom. This makes the tree branch look Round. (Form).

With a **Fascination with Observation**, take a moment and really study the coloring on the beak and do your very best to paint it in a similar way. Did you see how the bottom of the beak is darker than the top of the beak? Just like the tree branch, it's round, too!

The feet are like the letter "C" curving up a bit above the tree branch. Observe, one side is light gray and the other is dark gray which shows what again?? Roundness!!! That's right! (also called Form)

As we paint the rest of our **Toucan**, keep in mind the 'texture' of his feathers! Brush strokes should be up & down (vertical) on his body, because that's how his feathers grow!

Let's finish up our Toucan!

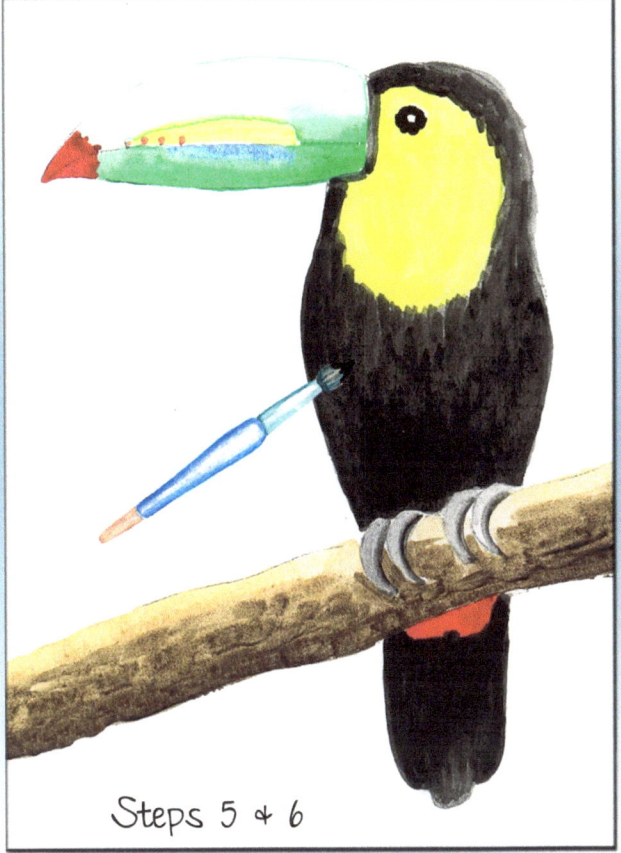

Steps 5 & 6

Below, I've drawn/painted examples of art by three Master Artists who also like to drawn/paint birds. These artists all work in different art 'styles', which means they see things in their own way and then paint or draw how they see it!

Pablo Picasso 1881-1973
Spanish
Look at his painting 'The Owl'

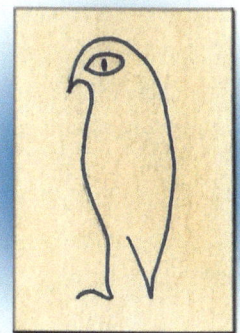

Picasso saw this bird using a simple line.
His Style - MODERN ART

Qi Baishi 1864-1954
Chinese
Look at his painting, 'Magpies & Plums'

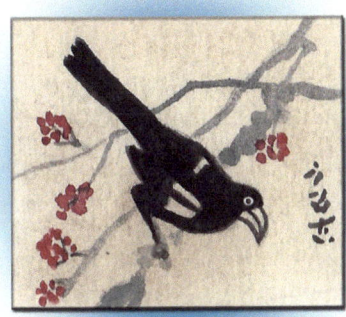

Baishi saw birds in a painterly way.
His style-CHINESE TRADITIONAL

John Gould 1801-1881
English
Look at his painting 'Toucans'

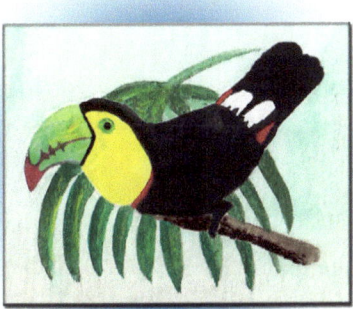

Gould sees birds in a realistic way.
His style - REALISM

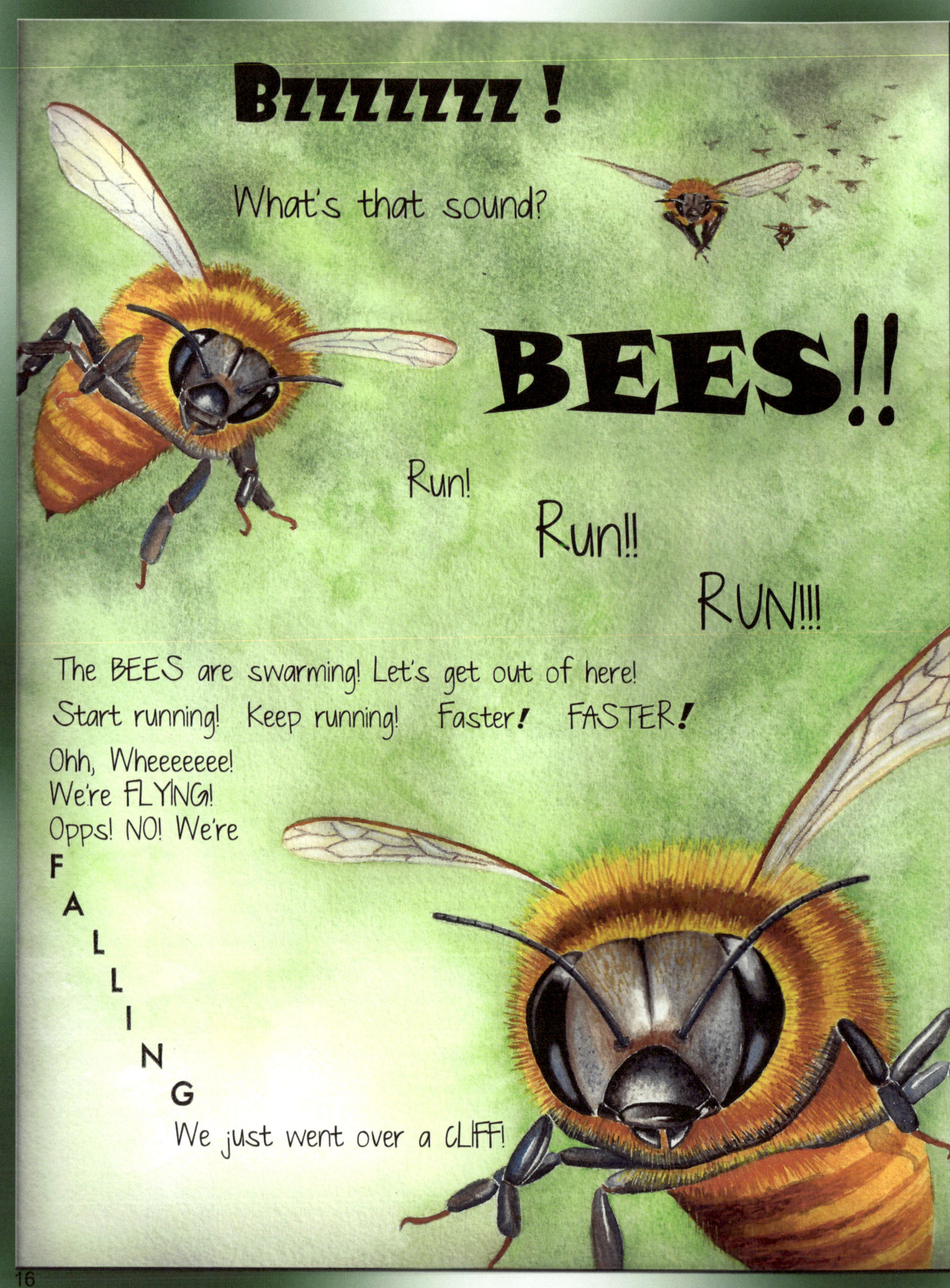

Bzzzzzz !

What's that sound?

BEES!!

Run!

Run!!

RUN!!!

The BEES are swarming! Let's get out of here!
Start running!   Keep running!   Faster!   FASTER!

Ohh, Wheeeeeee!
We're FLYING!
Opps! NO! We're

F
A
L
L
I
N
G

We just went over a CLIFF!

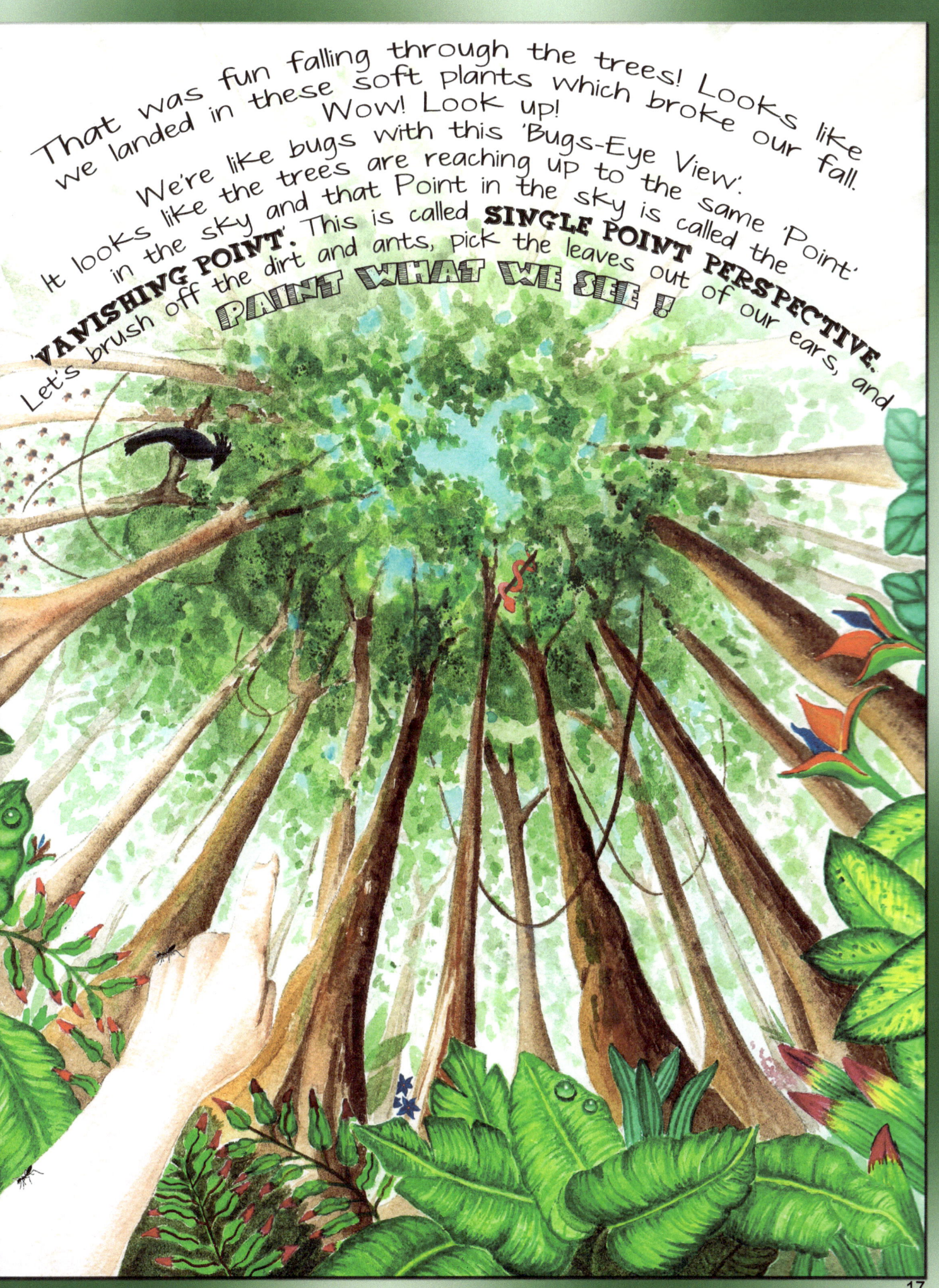

That was fun falling through the trees! Looks like we landed in these soft plants which broke our fall. Wow! Look up!
We're like bugs with this 'Bugs-Eye View'. It looks like the trees are reaching up to the same 'Point' in the sky and that Point in the sky is called the SINGLE POINT PERSPECTIVE. This is called 'VANISHING POINT'. Let's brush off the dirt and ants, pick the leaves out of our ears, and PAINT WHAT WE SEE !!

LET'S PAINT SINGLE POINT PERSPECTIVE
A BUGS EYE VIEW

NEEDED: Watercolor paper, palette, brush, water. Paints: green, yellow-green (mix yellow/green), brown & blue. And a pencil of course!

Follow the same instructions for setting up our palette in our previous projects. So, let's grab a pencil, look up at the trees, and

PAINT WHAT WE SEE !

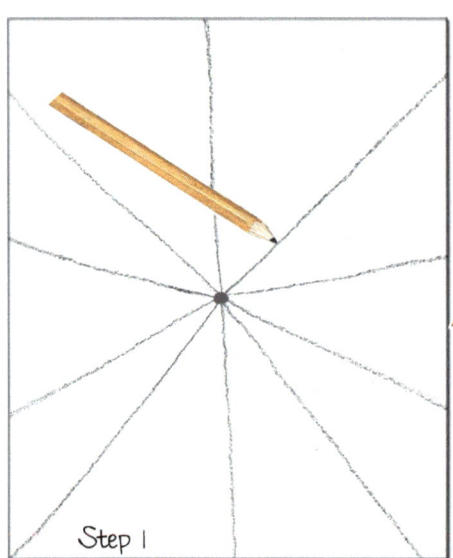

Step 1

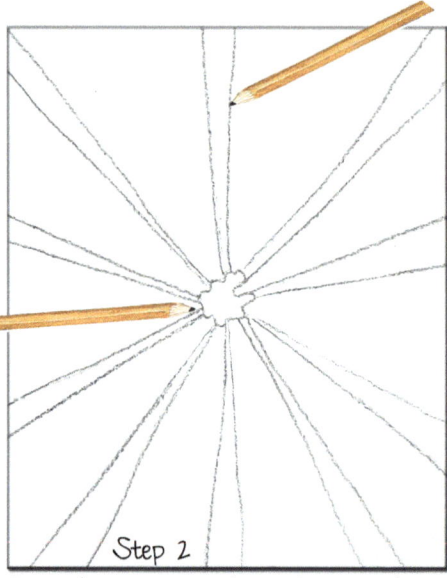

Step 2

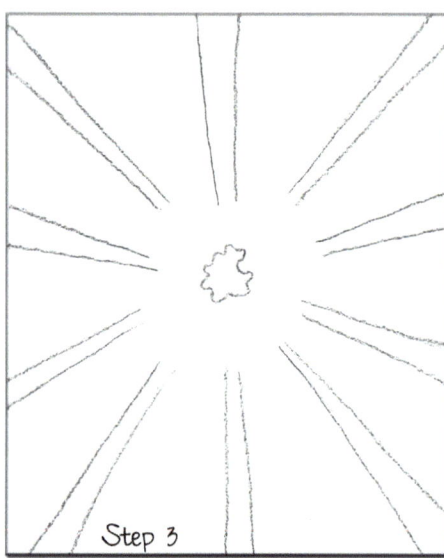

Step 3

Place a dot in the middle of your paper. Then, draw random lines coming out of the dot all around to the edges of the paper. This 'dot' is called The VANISHING POINT.

Next, draw a squiggly circle around the dot, then erase the dot. Now, add extra lines next to the lines we drew in Step 1 to make our tree trunks.

This step is the easiest! Just erase those lines closest to our squiggly circle...this is where our green leaves will be painted. The squiggly circle will be our blue sky.

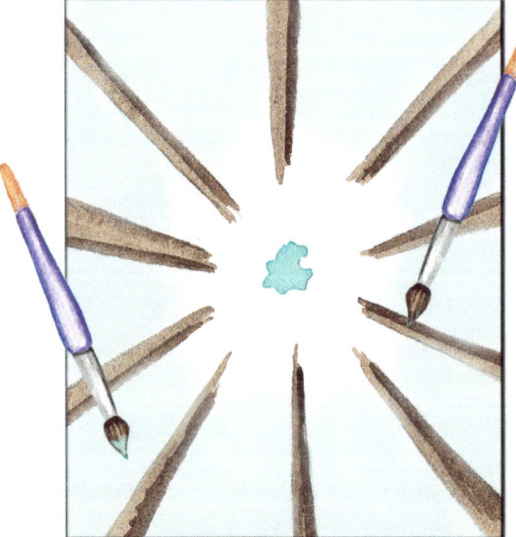

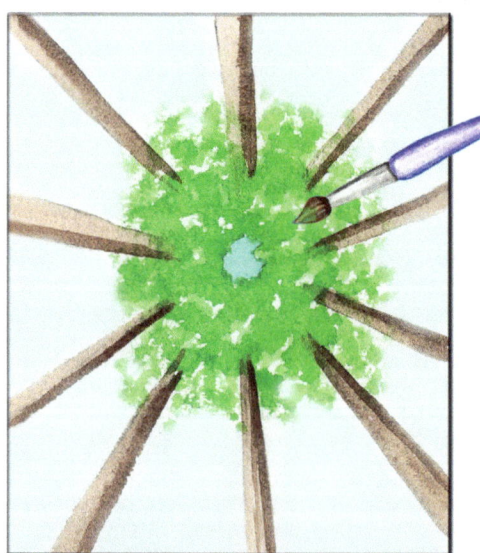

Paint the light blue (sky) just as you see in the example, Paint the tree trunks light brown first, then dark brown on 'one' side of each tree trunk as seen. This creates what?...Yes!!...Roundness or Form !!!!

With our yellow-green paint, use your brush to 'dab' on the paint. (This gives a leaf-like texture). Then, using the dark green paint, 'dab' that here & there over the yellow-green, this creates 'light & shadow' within the leaves.

SINGLE POINT PERSPECTIVE TREES

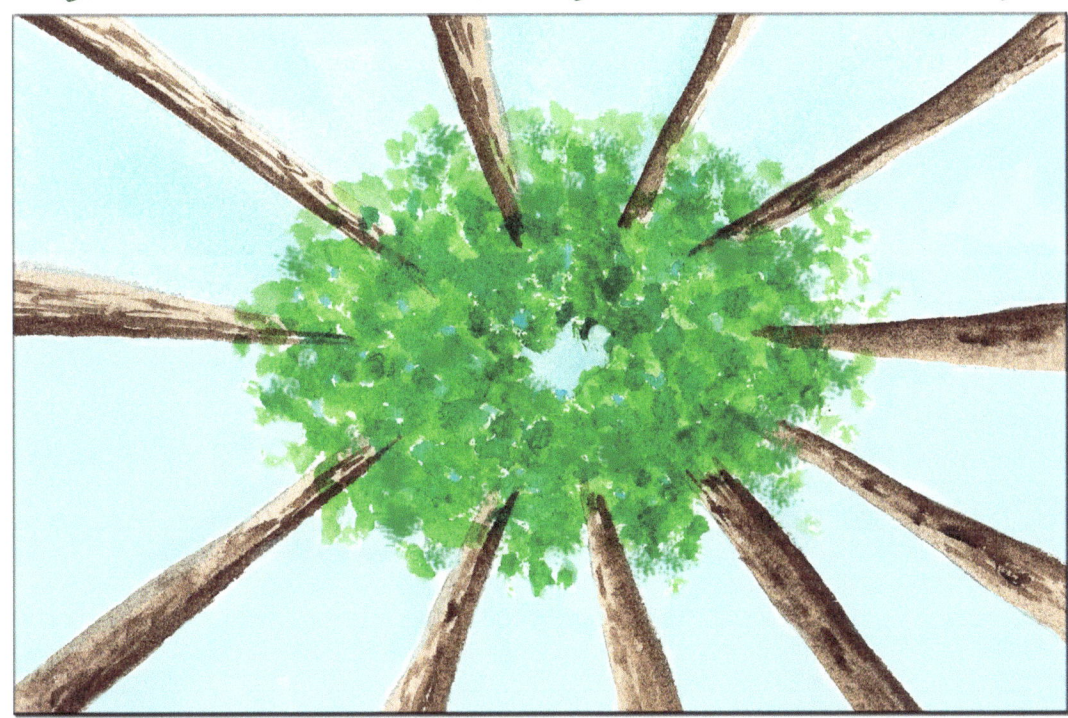

Let's add a little detail to our Bugs-Eye View of the trees... With our dark brown paint we can add some 'texture' to our tree trunks by making some chunky lines along the length. Remember how we added chucnky lines to the tree branch that the Toucan sat on?

Single Point Perspective is fun!

Below, I've drawn examples of artwork by three Master Artists who also use 'Single Point Perspective' in their artwork. Notice how using 'Perspective' brings the veiwer 'into' the artwork. These artists all paint in different art 'stlyes' which means they see things in their own way and then paint how they see it !

CLaUDE MONET 1840-1926
French
Look at his painting,
'Garden Path at Giverny'

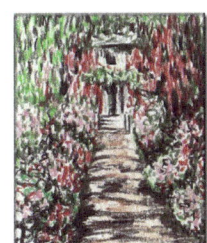

Notice how Monet's garden path & flowers seem to go to a single point in the painting. That's the Vanishing Point'! His style is FRENCH IMPRESSIONIST

COBBEGGIO 1489-1534
Italian
Look at his painting,
"Ceiling of Camera di San Paolo'

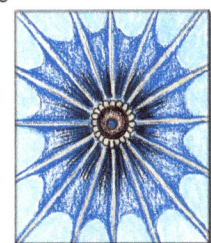

This painting is like our trees with the 'vanishing point' in the middle and all lines radiating out from it. Very Ornate !!! His style is ITALIAN RENAISSANCE

ALFBED SISLEY 1839-1899
English (lived in France)
Look at his painting
'Chemin de la Machine Louvecienne'

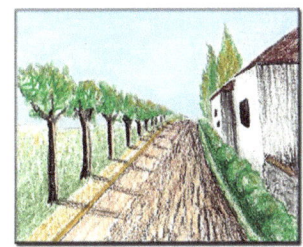

Notice the trees lining the road go from big to small as they dissappear into a point in the painting, the 'Vanishing Point'! His style is IMPRESSIONIST

These 3 works of art are painted by Jan Wood Harris in a style similar to the paintings listed.

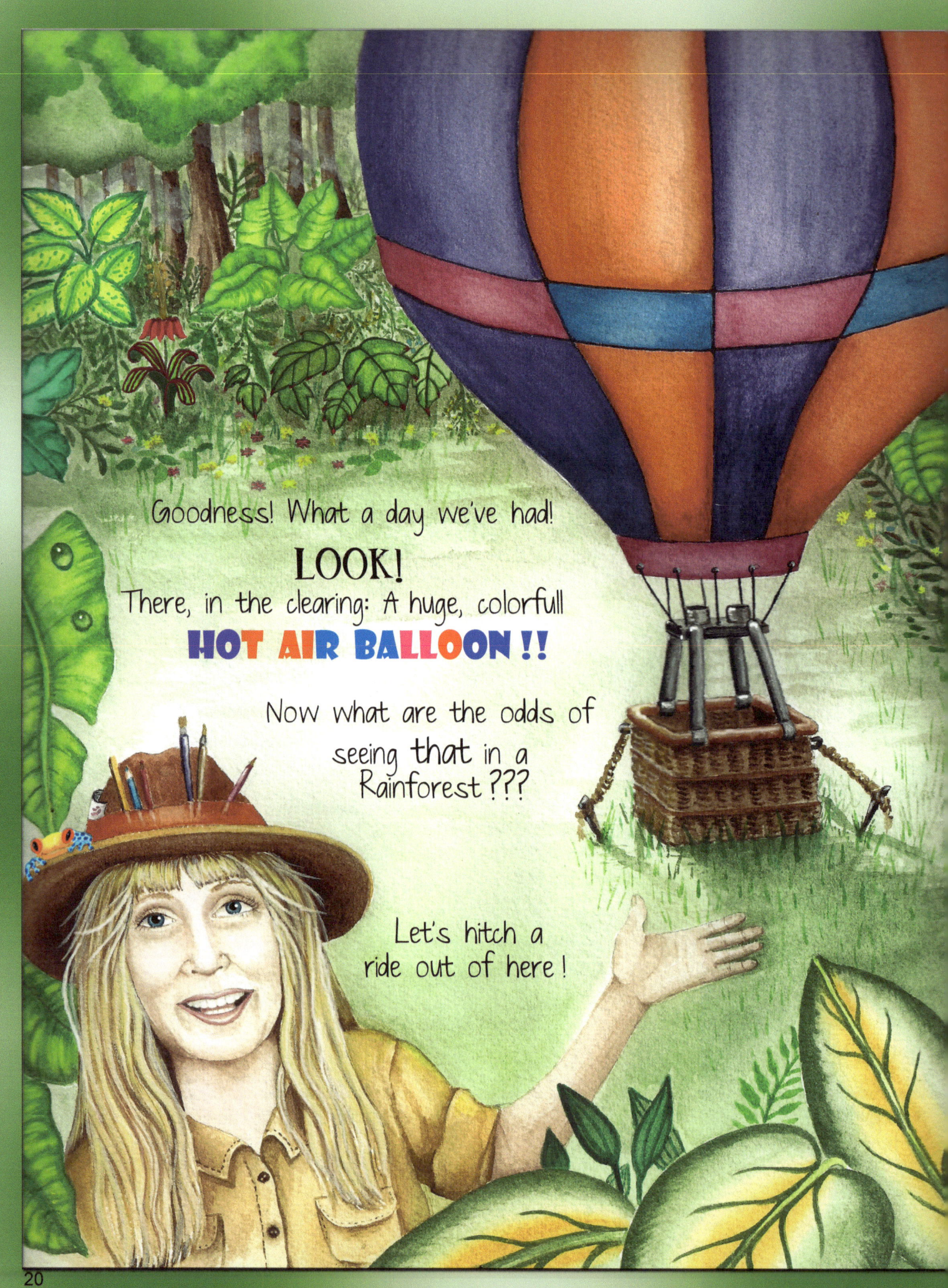

Goodness! What a day we've had!

LOOK!

There, in the clearing: A huge, colorfull

HOT AIR BALLOON !!

Now what are the odds of seeing **that** in a Rainforest ???

Let's hitch a ride out of here !

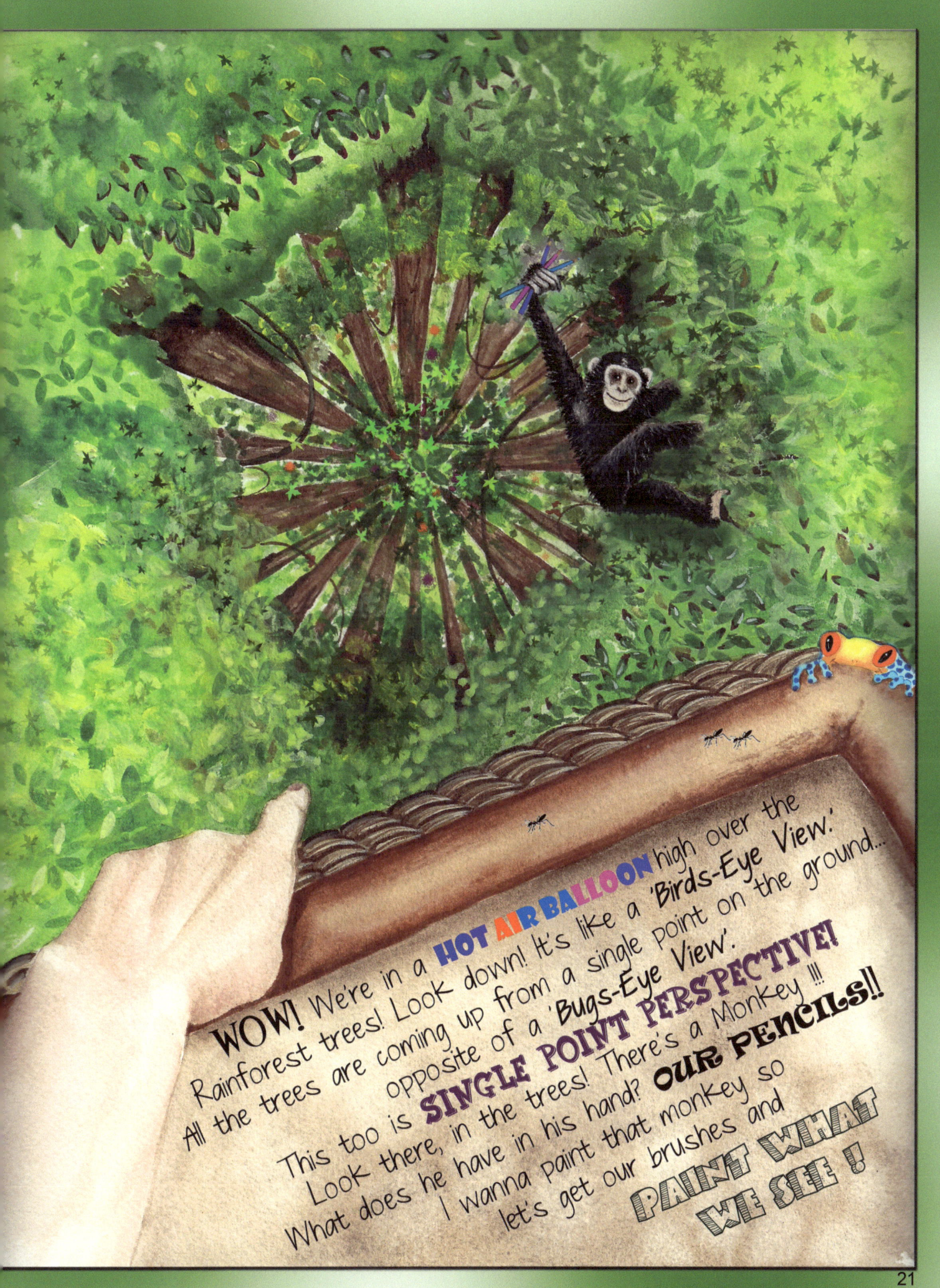

WOW! We're in a **HOT AIR BALLOON** high over the Rainforest trees! Look down! It's like a 'Birds-Eye View.' All the trees are coming up from a single point on the ground... opposite of a 'Bugs-Eye View'.

This too is **SINGLE POINT PERSPECTIVE!**

Look there, in the trees! There's a Monkey !!!
What does he have in his hand? **OUR PENCILS!!**
I wanna paint that monkey so let's get our brushes and

PAINT WHAT WE SEE !

LET'S PAINT THE SILLY MONKEY!

NEEDED: Watercolor Paper, palette, brush, & water. Paints: brown, black and white. And a pencil, of course!

Follow the same instructions for setting up our palette in our previous projects. Let's grab a pencil, and a brush, and

PAINT THE SILLY MONKEY!

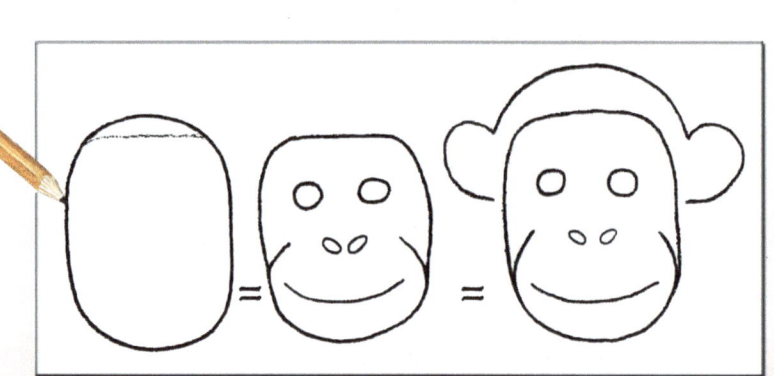

Start with a **fat** oval, then flatten the top. Half way down the oval, draw two curved lines to form his cheeks. Add his nostrils and eyes. Lastly, draw the top of his head and ears.

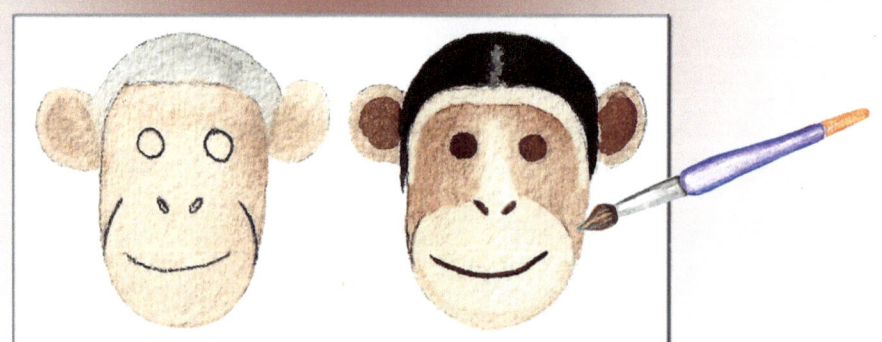

Now let's add some paint. Using light brown, color his whole face & ears. Be sure the brown is dry, then add the light gray to the top of his head. (Remember, more water gives a lighter color, less water gives a darker color.)

Once this is all dry, paint with a darker brown around his eyes & above his cheeks. Be sure to leave a 'ridge' unpainted around his forehead & along the length of his nose. Paint darker centers of the ears. Color in his eyes and nostrils, and use a small brush to paint a thin line for his mouth.

These are the colors of paint for your Palette ⇨

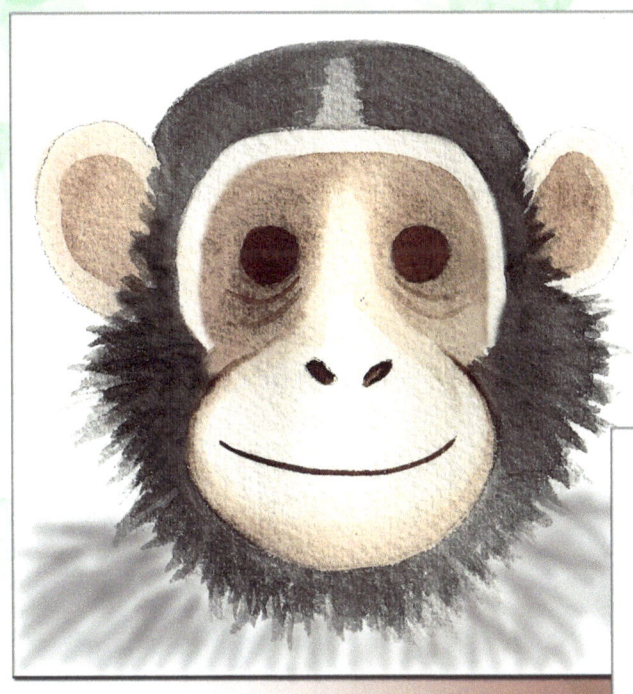

THE SILLY MONKEY

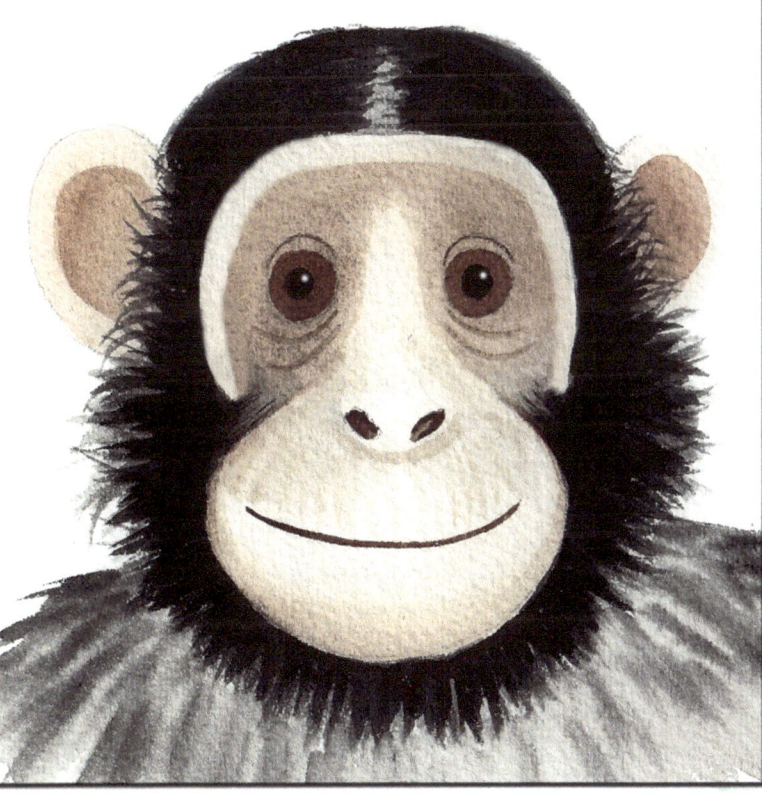

Now let's add some detail. Still using the light gray, paint the shoulders. Let dry. Using dark gray, (add a bit of black to your light gray; mix). Start painting the monkey's hair. Be sure your paint strokes start from the head out.

Use your creativity and add some leaves in the background like the one you learned to draw previously in our adventure.

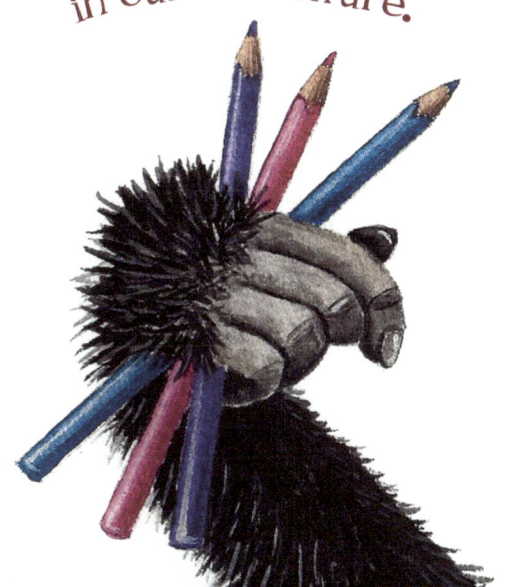

Make sure the paint is dry before proceeding. Using black paint (add a tiny bit of water to the paint). Go over the gray hair you just painted using the same technique. With a smaller round brush, paint the black center in the eyes. Then using brown paint, paint the thin curved lines under and over the eyes. Lastly, put a little white paint on the eyes to show a sparkle, and it's done!

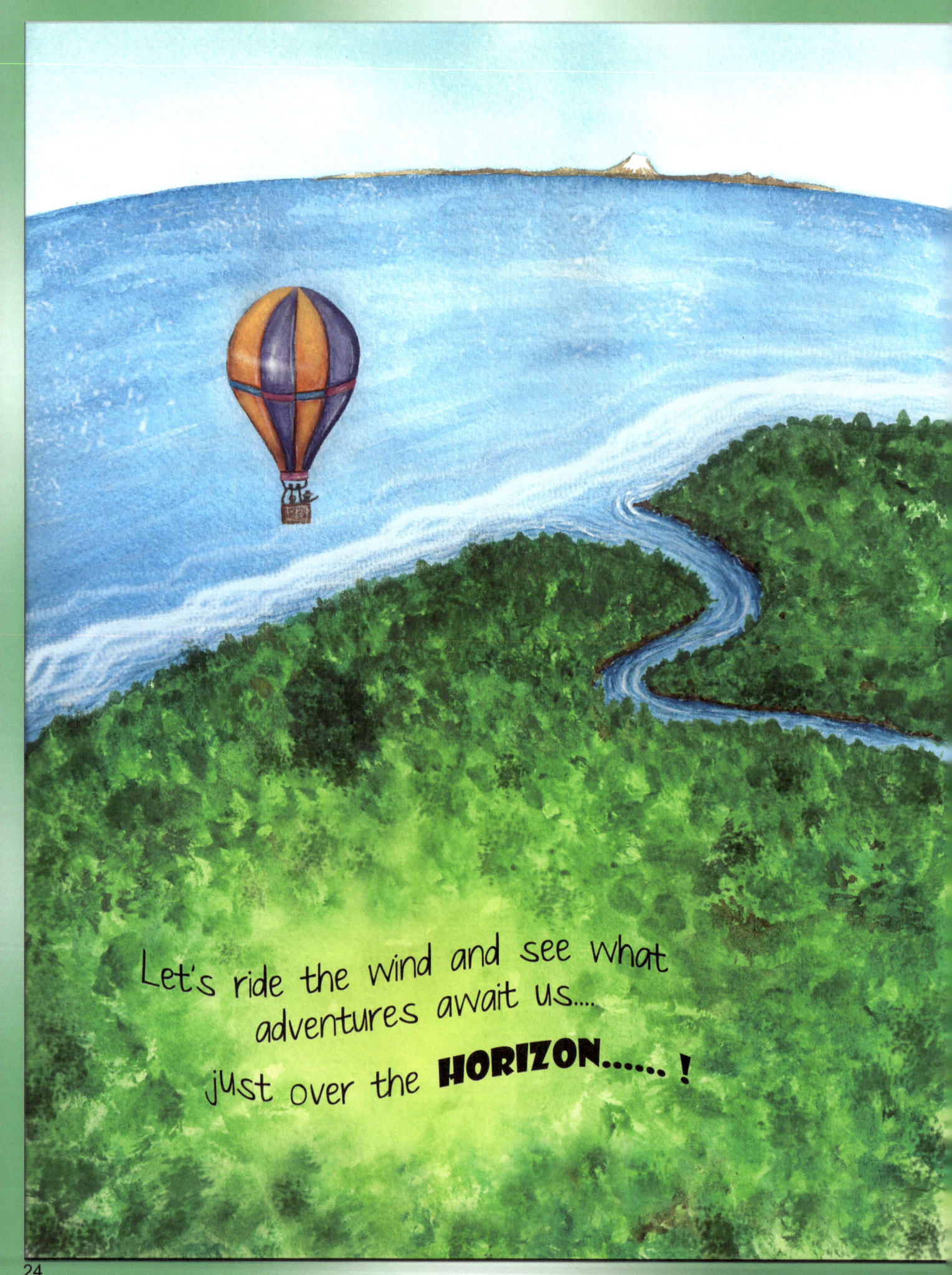

Let's ride the wind and see what
adventures await us....

just over the **HORIZON......** !

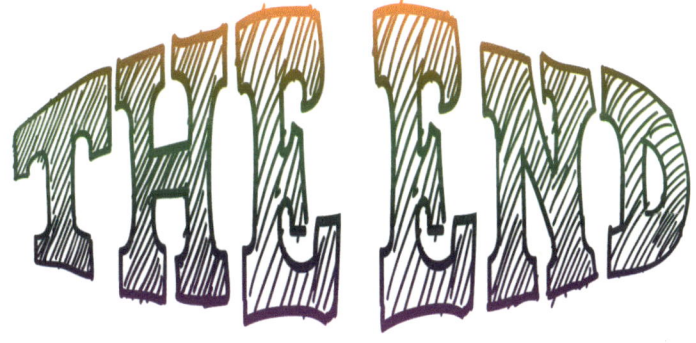

Just Kidding.
There's more.
Turn the page...!

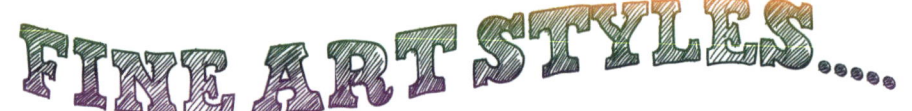

FINE ART STYLES.....

IMPRESSIONISM

Impressionism is a style of painting that began in Paris, France in the mid-1800's. These artists used many short brush strokes applying paint thickly, to create the idea, or impression of a subject. In other words, they were painting their 'impression' of what they were seeing. Impressionist painters were very interested in light and shadows. They studied how light changed the shadows on the subjects they painted. When you look up close at these paintings, often the paintings won't look like anything but a bunch of paint blobs. When you back away from it, though, you can see the whole picture. Primitiive style uses primitive images which are considered wonderfully child-like and dreamy.
Impressionist Painters named in this book: Claude Monet, Vincent Van Gogh & Alfred Sisley
Impressionists named in this book in the Primitive Style: Henri Rousseau & Pointillism Style: George Seurat.

REALISM & ROMANTIC REALISM

Realism was an art movement that began in France in the 1850's. Realists painted everyday people, situations, and objects, all in a "true-to-life" way. These artists simply drew or painted what they saw right in front of them. Romantic Realism was around the same time as Realism and they were very similar except that in this style the artist created people, situations and objects all in perfect, surreal and absolutely beautiful ways, almost dream-like and magical.
Realism Painter named in this book: John Gould
Romantic Realism Painter named in this book: John Constable

MODERN ART

Modern Art is a general term, used for most of the artistic creations in the late 19th century. Modern art refers to a new approach to art where it was no longer important to paint a subject as it was seen.   Instead, artists started experimenting with new ways of seeing, with fresh ideas about how to paint nature, people etc., often moving towards more abstraction.
Modern Artists named in this book: Georgia O'Keeffe & Pablo Picasso

SYMBOLISM

Symbolism started in the late 19th century. This style was somewhat opposite of realism. The painter favored expressing an 'idea or concept' using spirituality, imagination and a more dream-like scene. Realistically un-realistic, if you will!
Symbolist named in this book: Gustav Klimt

ITALIAN RENAISSANCE

Italian Renaissance began in the late 13th century and flourished from the early 15th to late 16th centuries, beginning in Florence, Italy. This was a huge movement in Europe which went through many stages. The painters of Renaissance Italy were often attached to particular royal courts and with loyalties to particular towns. Painters of this time and style paid huge attention to the use of Perspective and had very complex compositions. They also had a sophisticated use of light and shadow to create the illusion of depth, like you could walk right into their paintings!
Italian Renaissance artist named in this book: Correggio

CHINESE TRADITIONAL

Chinese painting is one of the oldest continuous artistic traditions in the world. Traditional painting is done with a brush dipped in black or colored ink. Oils are not used. The most popular materials on which paintings are made are paper and silk. The finished works can be mounted on scrolls, such as hanging scrolls or handscrolls.
Chinese Traditionalist named in this book: Qi Baishi

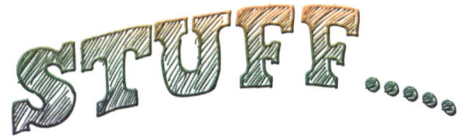

line

Line is like a dot that just keeps moving. Line is the most basic element of art. It can be thin, thick, squiggly, jagged, spiraly, or go this way or that!

VALUE

Value deals with the lightness or darkness of color, or the transition from black to white. A circle is made into a ball by gently moving from dark to light from one side to the other. This characteristic of value helps an artist create illusions of life like forms.

SHAPE & FORM & CONTOUR

Shape may be created of just a line or a solid area. Typical shapes that artists use are the circle, square, rectangle, & oval. There are also those shapes that are hard to say called the parallelogram, trapezoid, pentagon, hexagon, & octagon. Then, there are just those fun free-form shapes that might be curved or angular or just plain silly! Form can be round or curvy and the use of Value will help to create the illusion of Form. Contour lines show the edge of a form or a change in a surface, like a curved leaf.

SPACE

Space refers to the emptiness of areas between, around, above, below, or within objects.
This space is called **Negative Space**: the empty space between the shapes or forms.
And **Positive Space**: the shapes or forms that are drawn or painted.

COLOR

Color use in art has the ability to be bold & bright, simple or light, exciting or calming, to name a few. Colors are described in art in three ways;
Hue simply refers to a color's name – red, blue, pink, green, etc.
Value has to do with the color's lightness or darkness.
Intensity is how bright or dull it is.

TEXTURE

Texture in art is the way an object feels to the touch or looks as it may feel.
Rough, smooth, bumpy, lumpy, fuzzy, jagged, feathery, scaly, etc.

PERSPECTIVE ☆ DEPTH

Perspective is a way of creating the illusion of a three-dimensional space on a flat surface, such as paper or canvas. It's like looking at a painting on a wall as a window and looking through it to see the world as it is. It can get very technical (but fun!) with **Vanishing Points** (where all angled lines vanish into) and **Horizon Lines** (where the sky meets the land).
An artist can also create **Depth,** (like you can see way into a painting) by **Overlapping** objects such as hills & trees & people, using darker colors up close and lighter colors far away.

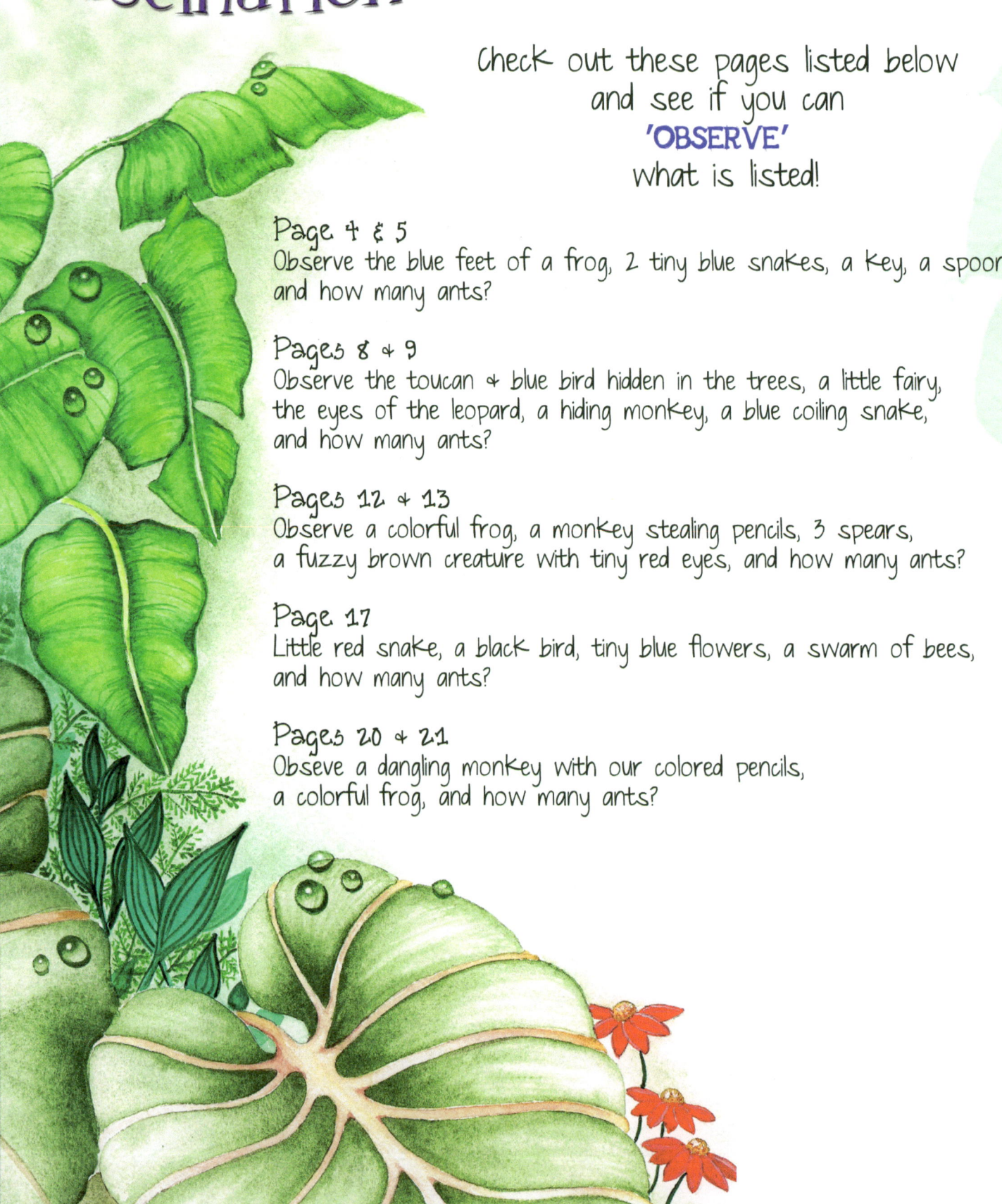

Fascination with Observation

Check out these pages listed below
and see if you can
'OBSERVE'
what is listed!

Page 4 & 5
Observe the blue feet of a frog, 2 tiny blue snakes, a key, a spoon,
and how many ants?

Pages 8 & 9
Observe the toucan & blue bird hidden in the trees, a little fairy,
the eyes of the leopard, a hiding monkey, a blue coiling snake,
and how many ants?

Pages 12 & 13
Observe a colorful frog, a monkey stealing pencils, 3 spears,
a fuzzy brown creature with tiny red eyes, and how many ants?

Page 17
Little red snake, a black bird, tiny blue flowers, a swarm of bees,
and how many ants?

Pages 20 & 21
Obseve a dangling monkey with our colored pencils,
a colorful frog, and how many ants?

RAINFOREST CROSSWORD PUZZLE

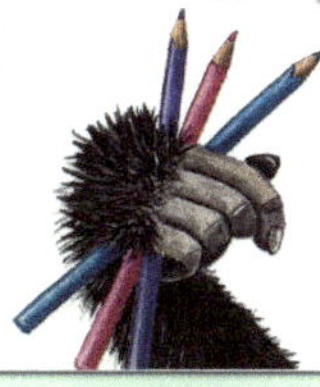

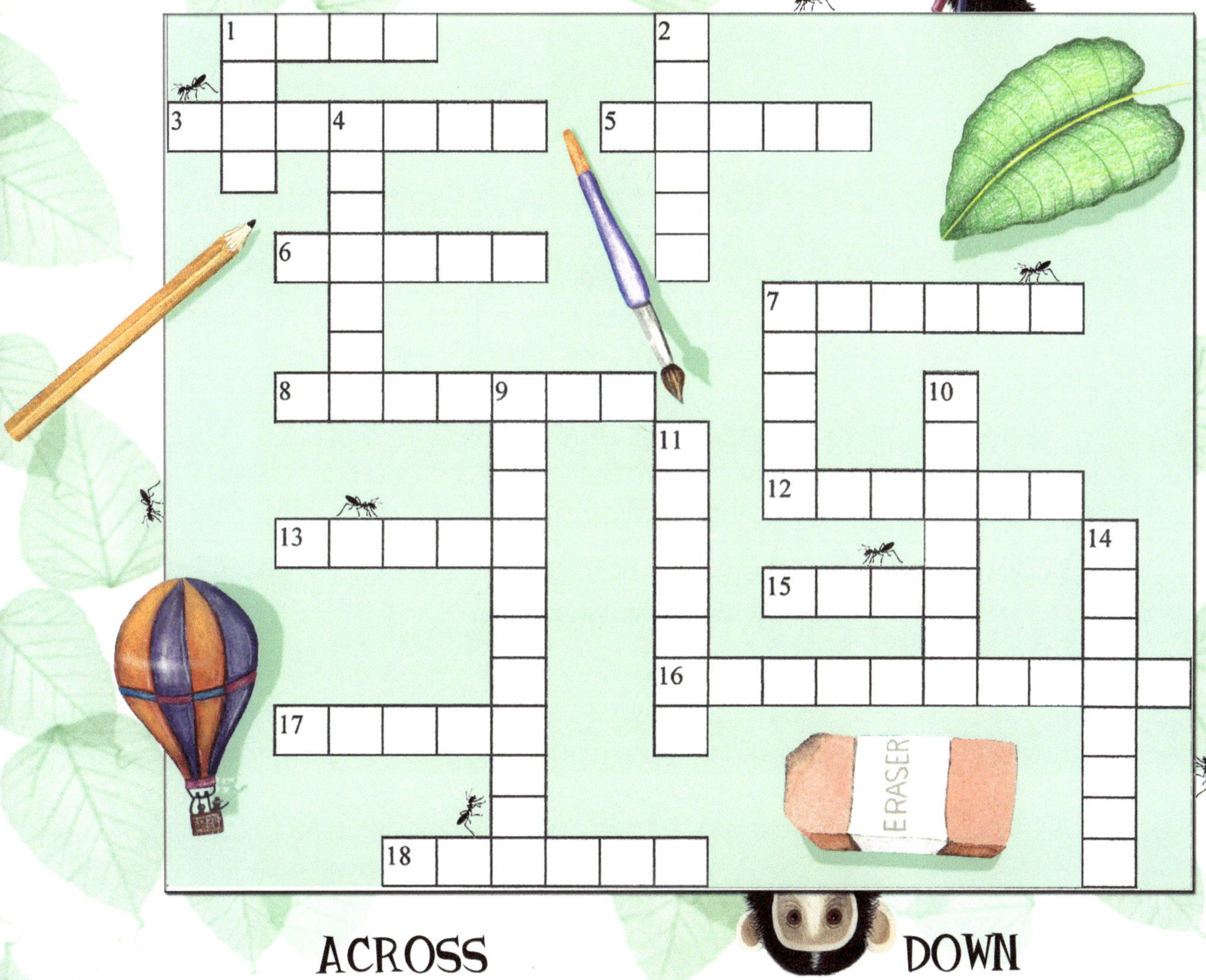

ACROSS

1. Can be thick or thin
3. A Dutch artist
5. Goes light to dark
6. Paint with this
7. Can draw with this
8. Filled with Hot Air
12. Has a big beak
13. Coils on branches
15. Tiny insects
16. A lot of wet trees
17. An Impressionist painter
18. Steals pencils

DOWN

1. Can sit under this
2. Takes lines away
4. A woman artist
7. Liquid color
9. A fascination with...
10. An abstract painter
11. Rough & bumpy
14. A Primitive Style artist

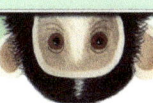

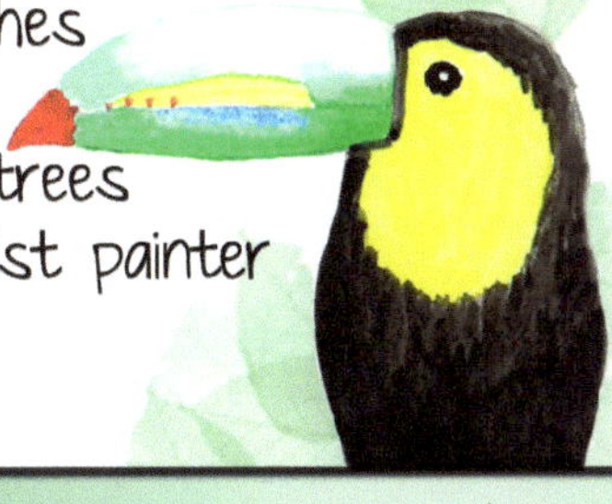

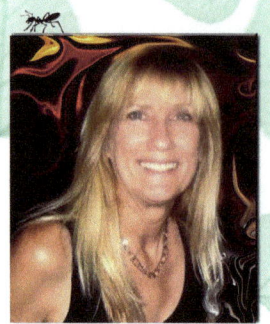

Jan Wood Harris is an accomplished painter/illustrator and has been sharing her knowledge and love of art through her teaching for many years now. This is her second illustrated children's book, her first being 'Ben the English Afghan Hound'.

Jan Wood Harris has two grown daughters, Madison and MacKenzie, and lives with her husband Robert in southern California. She continues to teach art and work on the next

'Ms Wood's Wild Art Adventures' in new and exciting places...

Keep in touch with 'Ms Wood' at www.janwoodharrisart.com

Puzzle answers

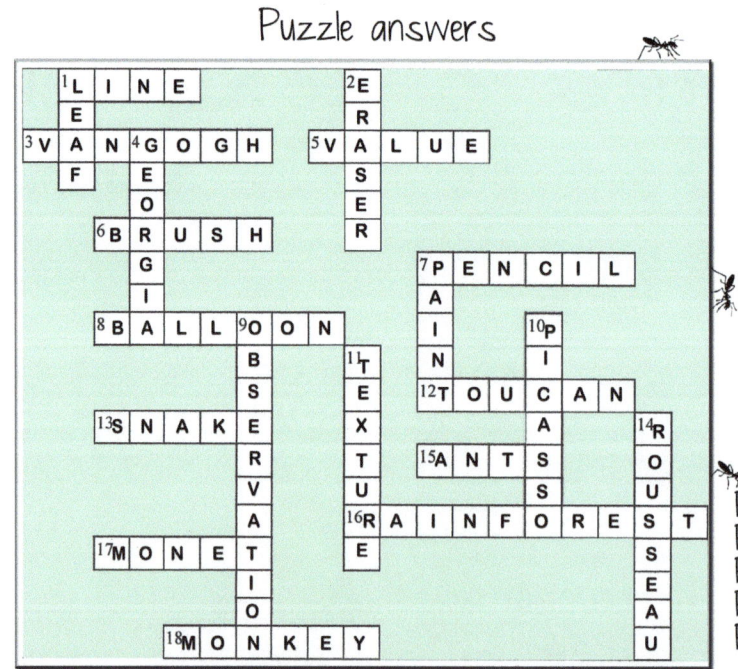

Page 4 & 5, three ants
Page 8 & 9, Eight ants
Page 12 & 13, nine ants.
Page 17, two ants.
Page 20 & 21, 3 ants.